WILL THIS COUNTRY SURVIVE?

A second war with England
1812-1815

Privately Published
July 2013
July 2022
Albuquerque, NM

ISBN-13: 9781491216071
ISBN-10: 1491216077

WILL THIS COUNTRY SURVIVE?

Our Family in the War of 1812
By
C. W. Cissna

Second Edit
2022

Books for Researchers
Available at Amazon.com

House of Cessna, Book One: The earliest research by
Howard Cessna, completed in 1903, has been
reproduced. Information from newer research
has been included.

House of Cessna, Book Two: Howard Cessna's work
"House of Cessna, Second Series" published in
1935, is reprinted here. Some newer information
is included.

House of Cessna, Book Three: A report of research
done in France. Research there is far from
complete. This is a starting point or future searches.

Early Cessna Farms: References and maps locating
farms established between 1739 and 1820.

Our Cessna Legacy: Analytical Biography of Major
John Cessna, with maps and 383 references.

Reconstructed Census: A cautionary recreation of the
family's First century in America. (Subject to
revision as we continue researching.)

Muster Call: A partial anthology of family members
who have served in U. S. branches of the Military.

Our Fifteen Minutes: Two hundred-fifty years of
humorous, sad, and inspiring newspaper articles
spotlighting family members in their moments
of fame or infamy.

Tri-Centennial Celebration and Cessna Reunion.
Outline of the 2018 National Cessna Reunion, with
and a guide for visiting the family's historical
sites in Pennsylvania.

Cessnas Gather: A summary report and journal of the
2018, from the Three Hundred Year National
Cessna Reunion.

Those Who Rest at Woods Cemetery: 2018 Survey of
Wood's Cove Methodist Protestant Cemetery in
Rainsburg, matched with obituaries for Cessna Family
members.

OUR AMERICA SERIES:
A history of America through slightly fictionalized
accounts of the lives of family members
Available at Amazon.com

Bury My Children in a Strange Land. Huguenot
refugee, Jean Le Cesna, transplanted his family
to American's wilderness in 1718.

The Reluctant American. Capt. Joseph Cissna survived 5
years captivity of with the Ottawa, six Indian
Wars, and the American Revolution.

Forgotten Courage. Pvt. Stephen Cessna/Cissna was among
the first men to volunteer in the American
Revolution. He was among the first men who
enlisted in the Continental Army and one of the first to
form Veteran's organizations.

Let Me Live in Peace. A chronicle of the struggles and
successes of Col. Charles Cessna, the highest
ranking Cessna during the American Revolution.

Tomahawks and Teacups. Jonathan Cessna was
kidnapped and adopted by the Ottawa during the
French and Indian War, and later died fighting
with Daniel Boone.

Will This Country Survive? The War of 1812 as it was
experienced by the various members of this
Cessna Family.

Where Can We Prosper? From 1810 to 1860.The
children of Capt. Evans Cessna survive epidemics and
financial recessions to build America's foundation.

A Nation and Family Divided. An anthology of 84
family members who fought on both sides of the
Civil War.

Civilizing a Pioneer Generation. After the Civil War,
Frontier Sheriff, George Sisney, faced down one
of the bloodiest vendettas in American History.
US Indian Agent, James Cisney investigated the
massacre at Wounded Knee and prevented a new
Indian War.

INTRODUCTION

The soldiers who fought the Revolution had long ago forgotten the horrors they had endured. They only remembered the glory of their experience. That is the part they retold.

The long cold nights of guard duty were forgotten. The blistering hot afternoons of waiting for an order to move in one direction or another were forgotten. The horror of soldiers disformed by cannon and musket ball, were abandoned to deep recesses in their souls.

Sleeping on wet ground; poor food; pay which was promised but never appeared; long exhausting marches with no apparent benefit; officers who had purchased their rank with money rather than military ability: all were faded from their memory. Days filled with the tedious labor of cutting firewood; building ramparts with hand shovels; digging latrines; marching in formation with men who cannot keep time: all of these were long forgotten.

Time had also erased the exasperation they had experienced at trying to get along with uneducated, pig headed, and self-centered backwoods men of poor hygiene. They had little choice about the men with whom they had been thrown into ranks.

Those characters who once provoked disgust and anger from them would forever be remembered as the finest sort of citizen soldier who ever lived.

They were heroes all!

The disillusionment they had know in their days of service was replaced with a deeply passionate patriotism.

These were hard men who had defeated the greatest military might on earth. They proudly wore their independence. They were quick to bristle at any insult, whether real or faint. And they preached these values to their children.

Those children would be the young lives thrown into the next war. Whether these young lives would be wasted, or become a precious investment in freedom, is a matter for each of us to decide.

But gaily dressed, and cloaked in patriotic fervor they would march towards a war that would resemble hell more than those glorious memories they had heard from their fathers.

In truth, each participant in the grand drama of the War of 1812 had his or her own motivations and self-serving ambitions.

This work does not seek to glorify this war or its participants in any way. There were members of my family who returned from the war in glory. Some returned broken. Some returned deeply disillusioned.

They were heroes all.

I have tried to tell their stories as accurately as possible. In doing so, I believe I have described the experience of most of our nation during this conflict.

These stories were created by matching pension and service records with histories of their units.

CHAPTER ONE
Prelude to War
A hungry lion was loose in Europe.

Napoleon was gobbling up land and countries faster than anyone had imagined possible. His military might was unprecedented. And wherever his army went they stole everything of value.

Art of every form, all government documents, and the best educated and most skilled citizens were all carried back to Paris. Napoleon intended it make it the capitol of the world. Everyone would have to travel to his capitol to see the most precious of human creations. Many of those stolen treasures still lie in the museums of Paris.

Great Britain was fighting for her life, both on land and sea. Napoleon seemed unstoppable and the English Parliament grasped at every resource to keep from being devoured.

America was a weak and inconsequential nation, as far as Parliament was concerned. So, stepping on American pride to commandeer resources seemed a small thing indeed.

British naval vessels were given orders to stop American ships whenever they happened to meet. Arms, food, and men would be taken from American ships and placed into service for the Royal Navy. England was in a desperate war!

Americans were livid at such thievery. But their complaints were a minor distraction for a Parliament in crisis. Americans became less and less inclined to remain neutral in the European War.

Even less important to Parliament were the affairs between Indian and Whites on the American Frontier. England needed money. The forests between the Ohio

River and Canada were rich with furs. England needed that money.

English policy was that the Indians were encouraged to keep all this land out of the hands of Americans, and continue harvesting as many furs as possible for the European fashion markets. It was in England's best interest to keep the profits flowing. If this meant providing the Indians with guns and ammunition, and buying the scalps of American settlers they killed with those weapons, so be it.

The Ohio Territory should be Indian lands as far as Parliament was concerned. The land-hungry Americans should stay south of the Great Lakes and the Ohio River.

Americans were gobbling up the lands of the Indian at an alarming rate.

Americans across the continent saw the policies of Great Britain as alarmingt. New England families were having their sons and fathers, kidnapped, and "enslaved" into the service of the King.

On the frontier, families were being massacred at the encouragement of (and with weapons provided by) the King. Resentment against England and the Indians grew exponentially with every terror inspiring attack.

Hungry wolves were fighting in Washington.

Congress was bitterly divided between the risk and benefits of war. But each week during 1811, the War Hawks gained increased influence. Political parties vied for power in an ugly contest where truth and character were the first to fall victim.

In truth, the young country was not prepared in any way for war.

The trained army was tiny, and widely scattered around the states. The navy was almost non-existent. The pool of trained officers to lead any military action was aged.

The younger officers were even more poorly trained than the men who would do the fighting. Most of the men who would become officers were politicians, not professional soldiers.

Reason dictated caution. But the passion for revenge was deep. War was at America's doorstep.

Those who least wanted war were the Canadians.

If England considered America to be tiny and insignificant, America looked with greater disdain upon the Canadians. Thomas Jefferson had remarked during his presidency that taking Canada from the British would involve little more than marching a small army there.

With less than 400,000 white citizens (300,000 in Lower Canada and 77,000 in Upper Canada), the British Provence seemed a dwarf to the 4.5 million Americans across her southern border.

And everyone knew that most of the people of Canada were really Americans who had moved there following the Revolutionary War. It was estimated that 3 out of 5 whites in Canada had moved there from the States of Massachusetts, New York, and Pennsylvania. Most considered "Canadian" to be a reference to the French settlers, not the Americans who had moved there 30 years earlier.

The common assumption of Americans was that those folks would be glad to be back in the Land of the Free. No one expected that they would become the formidable militia that came to fight against their American brothers.

What American pride would not let them see is the great distrust and hatred for the American brand of democracy that the people of Canada had.

It held the same venomous tone as communism would have for mid-twentieth century Americans, with just as much passionate hatred. For these former Americans, democracy turned the government over to the basest of mankind's greed and corruption. It pitted neighbor against neighbor in a ruthless anarchy of power.

Under English rule, the government was in the hands of educated aristocrats. In democracy, the government easily fell in the hands of the uneducated, the unprepared, and those filled with avarice. Any loud-mouthed lout who was good at lying could get himself elected. And once in power, they forgot all of the promises they had made.

The former Americans, now Canadians, called themselves "Loyalists" and believed fervently that a monarchy, balanced by Parliament, was the highest form of government humanity had achieved. Still wounded by the chaotic politics of the first two decades of America's development, most of our brothers to the North failed to see how the chaos of democracy provided any balance at all.

And just as today, it was hard to believe in the "checks and balances" promised by the US Constitution.

Though sharing a common background and language, Americans and the settlers in Canada were miles apart in political ideology.

Like estranged brothers, they were destined to meet on the battlefield.

CHAPTER TWO
Tecumseh's War

A hungry bear was loose in America.

The Shawnee and their fellow Native Americans had the most interest in war. Most of the Eastern Tribes were territorial and had a clear idea of which land was "theirs."

The American government simply assigned ownership of this land to them, then purchased it away, or seized it by right of victory in war. Most treaties were made with a small number of natives and did not represent all of the tribes who considered this their land.

Now they felt their land had been stolen. Ownership of the land then passed to Congress by way of the questionable treaties. Congress then sold the land at an enormous profit to settlers.

Government land selling for $2 an acre may not sound like huge profits. But when considered that some of that land was purchased from the natives for less than $.25 an acre, Congress had found a significant source of revenue.

George Washington told Congress it was much wiser (and less expensive) to just buy the land from the tribes rather than win it in war. Congress agreed. The government had been slowly purchasing millions of acres from one tribe after another.

The treaty agents did not pay close attention to how the natives viewed ownership. For example: the Iroquois Nations of upper New York sold all of Kentucky to Congress, even though no Iroquois lived there. In past years, they had conquered the Shawnee, and felt they had a right to sell the Shawnees' land to the whites.

In truth, the Shawnee would never benefit from any land sale. Repeatedly they had the land they lived and hunted on, sold out from under them by other tribes.

Of all the Eastern Tribes, the Shawnee were nomadic. They did not live in one area long enough for the white man to consider them in possession of it. So, the Shawnee were seldom invited to land-purchasing conferences.

Shawnee philosophy was that the land belonged to no man, yet was available to all men to survive on. The concept of selling something you did not, and could not, own, was repugnant to them.

Their resentment grew with every land purchase made by the Americans.

From among the Shawnee emerged a powerful leader. Tecumseh was a respected warrior chief and a phenomenal orator. Supported by his brother Tenskwatawa, "The Prophet," he began a campaign to unite the tribes.

Tecumseh had received a very specific vision and prophecy from "The Great Spirit." The power it promised was enticing to every warrior of every tribe.

His message was simple and effective: if the Indian continued to deal with the white man as individual tribes, they would soon be driven from the earth. The land-hungry Americans would eventually destroy the life which all native peoples had known.

The Great Spirit had promised there was but one last chance to save the red man from oblivion. It meant all tribes should come together under one giant native alliance, and declare war at the same time. Fighting as one giant army, they could drive the white man back into the sea.

But working together was not easy for the tribes. There were long histories of betrayal and mistrust between them. And under Indian government, each warrior was an independent authority.

Each man had the right to vote if he went to war or sought peace. Each man followed his own heart. Among the Iroquois, men could not go to war until the women had voted their approval.

When individual warriors banded together for war it had always been for very short-lived battles, not for prolonged organized conflicts. They fought as individuals, not as a coordinated unit like the white soldiers.

Most War Parties organized for a mission which lasted a few weeks. It was unheard of for them to engage in a war which might take years.

To prove that his vision had really from the Great Spirit, and that his message was true, Tecumseh offered a remarkable miracle.

For two years he traveled the continent, on both sides of the Mississippi River, visiting village after village. He preached his message and vision before dozens of warriors at a time, tens of thousands in total.

At each village, he left the elders a carefully prepared bundle of sticks. Each village had the same instructions. Every night one of the sticks was to be burned in the fire. On the last night, when only one stick (the only stick painted red) was left, they were to look into the sky for a sign.

The last stick, "the Red Stick," was then to be broken into thirty pieces. One piece was to be burned in the fire each night, until only one was left.

On the night that the last piece of the red stick was burned, the land would give them such a sign as had never been seen before.

Then all Indian peoples would know that the Great Spirit wanted them to go to war.

In the North, it was called Tecumseh's War.

In the Southern States, it was called the Red Stick War. The goal was that it would not end until every European had died or left these shores.

For the entire year of 1811, Tecumseh was in motion, traveling from village to village. Already a thousand warriors had answered his call and gathered at his War Camp in Prophet's Town along the Wabash River. Another four hundred or so followed him on his tour.

White setters watched in terror as large groups of warriors passed through the woods around them. William Harrison, Governor of the Indiana Territory, became alarmed by the considerable number of warriors at Prophet's Town, just a few days north of the capital at Vincennes.

It was obvious to everyone that war was coming. It was equally obvious that the Shawnee brothers of Tecumseh and The Prophet were at the center of it.

On November 16th of 1811, the next-to-last stick was thrown into the tribal fires. Only the red stick remained in each camp.

About midnight, a meteor entered the atmosphere over the central Rockies. As the heat of entry grew, so did its brightness. It traveled in a straight course from due west to due east. It could be clearly seen over all North America, and was recorded by both white and red observers.

As it crossed the Mississippi River, it exploded into three large pieces and thousands of little ones. From what one might describe as a firework starburst, three bright pieces streaked across the sky, making what every native recognized as the sign of the panther. Thousands of lips uttered the name "Tecumseh" (leaping panther).

The first of the two promised signs had arrived.

Every warrior was in awe of the miracle they had witnessed. Chiefs began to break the red stick into thirty pieces. Braves from every tribe began to head north to join the magnificent army that Tecumseh would lead. Thousands more hesitated for the second sign.

Each night another piece of the Red Stick was burned. They waited.

On the last night, the chief of each village dropped the final piece into the fire. Very few would sleep as they waited to see if Tecumseh's prophecy would come true.

Just before midnight, near the tiny Mississippi River town of New Madrid in the Missouri Territory, the earth shook itself as never before. The largest earthquake ever reported in North America stuck the continent.

The Mississippi erupted in wild erratic ways, sinking boats, and washing away homes along the river. A large section of land in Kentucky just sank. The river flooded in to create Horseshoe Bend Lake in just three hours.

In the Ohio River and many of its tributaries, the water ran backwards for several hours before resuming its normal flow. In native towns, warriors were knocked to the ground and their houses collapsed.

In Kentucky and Ohio, log cabins were knocked apart and stone chimneys were shaken lose. Church bells rang without human hands as far away as Pittsburgh. In Washington, D.C., several buildings sustained damage from the shaking.

Every soul, red and white, was startled awake at the noise created by livestock and wild animals. Flocks of birds were shaken from their roost only to fly around wildly trying to find safe rest in the dark. On the plains of Kansas and Nebraska, large herds of bison were knocked to the ground, and rose only to be knocked down again.

Every part of, and every person in America was aware of the event. Every red man knew it to be a sign from their creator that now was the time for war. No one had ever seen or heard of such an event.

This time, lips both red and white uttered the name "Tecumseh."

Prophet's Town sat at the juncture of the Tippecanoe Creek and the Wabash River. A creation of Tecumseh and his brother, Tenskwatawa, it was like no Indian town before it. It was a multi-national warrior's camp of magnificent size.

In the fall of 1811 slightly over 1000 warriors of various tribes made up its population. Some were from as far away as Georgia. It was the most diverse gathering of tribes ever recorded.

It had but one purpose. It was the largest war camp ever known in Indian history.

The British government in Canada had provided them enough food and materials to equip an army four times its current population. Tecumseh was expecting to lead at least 4-5 thousand braves in a war to exterminate the Americans.

Things were progressing well towards such an event.

But William Henry Harrison managed to foil his plans.

Spies informed Harrison of what was happening in Prophets Town. He had only 250 regular soldiers and about 90 cavalry men at his disposal, and he knew he was badly disadvantaged should the Indians bring the attack to him.

Taking the offensive seemed the only prudent thing to do.

From his capital of Vincennes on the Wabash River in Indiana Territory, he sent word to Kentucky for mounted militia volunteers. With amazing speed 700 Kentuckians, hungry for revenge on the red man, appeared at his door.

Marching up the Wabash in October, Harrison camped his force just one mile from Prophets Town, and waited. He had his men dig defenses and prepare to be attacked. This gave him great tactical advantage.

Tecumseh was still traveling and recruiting warriors. But he had left strict orders that if they were approached by an American Army, the Indians were to fall back in the forest and not give fight.

Tecumseh insisted that the fight must wait for the day of coordinated attack.

Tenskwatawa, however, saw this as his opportunity to ascend in leadership and power. Despite the protests of Tecumseh's lieutenants, he was able to convince the braves gathered in Prophet's Town to attack the American troops before dawn on November 7, 1811.

But the first sign predicted by Tecumseh was still 4 days away. It was too early according to his plan.

Tenskwatawa announced to the gathered warriors that he had received a vision from the Great Spirit.

All Indians would be invisible to the white man. They would be able to casually walk among them and strike them dead with just war clubs and tomahawks.

Soon after the battle began, when warriors were dropping in the usual way, it became apparent that his vision was false.

Even though the Americans suffered more casualties during the fighting than the Indians, the morale of the natives was devastated. They began to doubt the entire prophecy of Tecumseh. Most simply went home.

Harrison's army destroyed Prophet's Town and burned all of the food and materials collected for the war to come. It was a crippling blow to the momentum Tecumseh had worked so hard for.

As word of the defeat reached the various villages, many began to doubt the words of Tecumseh. The second of the two signs had not yet come.

Instead of a large native army suddenly taking to the field against unprepared American settlements, war began in a much less effective way.

Angry and disappointed warriors, on their way back to their homes, sought revenge on isolated American settlers up and down the frontier.

Reports began to flood from the west of lone hunters, or entire families, being found butchered throughout Indiana, Ohio, Kentucky, and Michigan. The attacks were uncoordinated and had no military effectiveness.

However, they created terror among the Americans and served to alarm and arm the population. This denied Tecumseh the element of shock and surprise he had planned for.

The Battle of Tippecanoe, and the seven months of what became known as Tecumseh's War, or the Red Stick War, should be included as the opening chapter of the War of 1812.

Congress declared war on Great Brittan on June 18, 1812. But everyone on the American frontier knew they had been fighting a war with England's Indian allies since November 7.

CHAPTER THREE
River Rouge
November 1811

Looking into the old man's eyes, it was impossible to tell how old he was. From the feebleness of his walk, and the depth of his cough, it was plain that he would not become much older than he was.

From the coloring of his costume, and the puckered seams of his moccasins, it was clear that he was Pottawatomie. His people had removed from this region of Michigan Territory almost 15 years ago.

Two young braves stood beside him, flanking him as if to catch him if he stumbled. They had brought him over six hundred miles of lakes and rivers from their home in Wisconsin to this section of River Rouge a short way from Fort Detroit.

To say their appearance caused quite a stir would be an understatement.

John Cissna had been interrupted from cutting wood by his wife, Jane. "John, you had better come quick."

From their farm on the south side of River Rouge, they had a clear view of the cabin built by John's father, Captain Joseph Cissna, 25 years earlier.

His father and mother were both gone. Joseph had married a second time, and his four youngest sons now lived there in a sort of bachelor house. It was a shoddy excuse for a home which would have given their mother fits to witness.

Joseph Jr., Stephen, David, and Evans Cissna did not possess one domestic skill among them. The degenerated state of their childhood home was ample proof of that fact.

Jane and John watched along with dozens of other River Rouge inhabitants as the dugout canoe and its three occupants came to rest in front of the old Cissna homestead.

With great care the young men helped the aged warrior from the canoe. He struggled to a point in front of the house and sat down, waiting to be greeted.

It was custom that the oldest of the Cissna sons would come forward to greet this visitor. But William was away on a trade journey.

It would take a month before the Cissna family discovered that William had already been murdered by some of Tecumseh's warriors.

Being the next oldest of the Cissna sons, it was John's duty to greet this visitor. He quickly crossed the river in a small skiff. Jane had handed him a special bag with the tools he would need for this encounter.

Walking slowly to the trio of guests, John did what he had watched his father do many times in the past. His father had been brothers with this old warrior's people. They had come many times to Joseph Cissna's home.

John sat cross-legged in front of the old man. With slow and deliberate moves he pulled a long pipe from the sack and filled it with tobacco. Saying nothing, he lit it and puffed deeply.

Eventually, he handed the same pipe to his visitors. Just as carefully they took turns puffing deeply. Then, with cupped hands, they pulled the exhaled smoke back over themselves as an act of spiritual cleansing.

When the old man finally spoke, John was sure he recognized some familiarity to the mannerisms. He was not sure how, but he felt certain that he had met this man before.

Perhaps, he was one of the dozens of Indians who had come to stand in honor of his father when he passed nine years earlier.

"Are you the son of Yabe'waboyan?" asked the old man in broken English.

John Cissna recognized the name his father had been given by the Pottawatomie people at his adoption into the tribe in 1757.

Joseph Cissna had been kidnapped from Shippensburg, Pennsylvania when just 10 years of age. Brought to this very forest in Michigan, he was eventually adopted as one of their own. Joseph had become a warrior before he escaped back to his white family five years later.

Following the American Revolution, Captain Joseph Cissna had led a group of settlers back to this lush place. He negotiated with the Pottawatomie for the group to purchase farms along this very river.

John and his brothers had been raised here. They each knew the Indian side of their father. They knew his Indian name: "Elk Skin."

"I am," answered John. "And I welcome the fellow tribesman of my father. May I ask what has caused you to make such a long journey?"

The old warrior would not tell John that he had begged his grandsons to take him on one last visit to his birthplace. His father and grandfather were buried a few hundred yards from the ground on which they sat.

The old warrior had wanted to make a complete circle of life back to his beginning place. Somehow, he hoped the journey would help him answer some troubling questions.

John would also never know that this man would die a few days after this visit, and be secretly buried in his ancestral lands by the grandsons who adored him so much.

What John did learn was more than he could accept.

"War is coming. Soon." The old man stated these words in a flat tone. Their truth and meaning required no additional emphasis. "The warriors who will come to this place seek the death of all white Americans."

John did not know how to respond, so the old man continued.

"These are men who have no memory of your father. And your family now lives under the flag of the United States. You no longer serve the English King.

"You will be seen as Americans, and the enemies of all red peoples. You must leave this place, or the seed of my brother Yabe'waboyan will vanish from the earth."

His message delivered, and needing no answer, the old man awkwardly rose and slowly returned to his canoe.

John was mystified that he should receive such a visit, with such news. He had no way of knowing that the man before him was his father's adopted brother.

Three years younger, this man had looked up to Joseph Cissna with admiration and love. Joseph had saved the boy from several disasters. And now the old man was paying his final debt to his white brother.

The canoe moved silently further up the River Rouge. Immediately, people up and down the river began to make their way to John's home and ask for explanations.

None of the farmers in Springwells Township was surprised that war was coming. Rumors had abounded for months. But it was shocking that John Cissna would get such a personal warning.

The people began to debate this event and what might be done about it. Opinions and options varied widely.

But the response was crystal clear for Jane Glass Cissna. As a child, she had witnessed her parents and siblings murdered along the Ohio River during the last Indian War. Taken captive, she and a younger brother had been rescued and raised by adoptive parents at Fort Detroit.

She knew there was only one acceptable response to the threat of a new Indian war: **leave**!

"We have to go. Now!" she told her husband. There was no room in her attitude for argument or debate.

John and Jane Cissna had three small children. Elizabeth was five, Joseph Glass Cissna was three, and Robert Glass Cissna was not quite five months. Her nightmares of the massacre never having left her completely, Elizabeth knew she must take her children far from this place.

It was far more than distant memories which motivated her desire to move. The winds of war on the American continent blew strongest in the area around Detroit. She was but one of many mothers contemplating the terror just over the horizon.

Jane Glass-Cissna was correct in her assessment of the situation. William Cissna would never return from that trade mission. He was murdered by a Potawatomie raiding party less that 20 miles from his home.

The group of farms along the River Rouge was actually closer to the British Fort Malden at Amherstburg, Canada, than they were to their own Fort Detroit. Tensions had been high between the countries for a dozen years.

In the past year, large groups of native war parties had been moving back and forth across the border, frequently using River Rouge as their highway, gliding ominously past the Cissnas' front door on the dark river.

As they returned from Canada, most of those natives were carrying brand new muskets. Some of them had even held their weapons high and shook them in warning to the white settlers as they passed.

At that time, William Hull, Governor of Michigan, had been recalled to Washington, D.C. for "instructions." Only the most naïve thought his purpose was anything to plan a war.

But Jane's greatest concern was her husband's occupation. The Cissna men were *Voyageurs*.

In addition to farming, William, John, and James Cissna traveled the back rivers of the wilds to trade goods with Indians for the precious commodity of furs. Such ventures frequently took them to the most isolated and dangerous parts of the forest.

William had been on one such business trip when the old Warrior visited the Cissna home.

In December of 1807, the United States adopted the Embargo Act. It was designed to punish England and France for not respecting the neutrality of American shipping, by stopping all trade with either country.

But the U.S. had no navy to enforce the embargo, so the only effect it had was to cripple honest tradesmen like those along the River Rouge.

In 1808, John Jacob Astor arrived in Detroit. John Jacob had a brilliant plan and was destined to become a multi-millionaire and founder of the Astor fortune. He incorporated the American Fur Company in New York City, and founded another corporation, the Southwest Fur Company, in Canada.

Every shipment of his furs had officers from each corporation. If they were stopped by American Officials, the American Fur Company representative stepped forward and claimed they were American goods.

If he were stopped by the British, his representative from Southwest Fur Company stepped forward and claimed they were British goods. The lines of the embargo became invisible to his multi-national conglomerate.

Arriving at Detroit, he began to recruit dozens of *Voyageurs* and traders to reach deep into the woods to every Indian. Since individual traders had little chance of success, most quickly joined John Astor's company.

The fur trade once again began to flourish and cash flowed into the Michigan Territory.

The Cissna family and the community along the River Rouge were well suited for his employment.

Joseph Cissna had been raised as a Pottawatomie from the age of 10-15. He spoke easily with Indians, the French, and Americans.

Captain Cissna taught his sons the ways of the woods and a respectful way to deal with the red man. The Cissna family in Michigan lived easily in the cultural twilight between the red and white man.

William, John, and James Cissna had all the attributes John Astor sought.

They were among the first to join the staff of the American Fur Company. John Burbank was among several other men from the River Rouge settlement who joined with them.

Editor's Note: John Burbank married the widow of William Cissna. When John and James Cissna moved to Holmes County, Ohio during the War of 1812, John Burbank, William's widow, and children, came with them. He established a trading post on the Killbuck Creek at a place that now bears his name: Burbank, OH. When Johanna died in Holmes County, James Cissna would be named guardian to protect the interest of William's children in his estate on the River Rouge.

William Cissna had been assigned to the streams of western Michigan. That was where he met his fate.

John and James Cissna were assigned to work in the Ohio Rivers which emptied into Lake Erie's southern shore. Specifically, they made frequent trips up the Black River to where a short portage carried them to Killbuck Creek and the tribal lands of the Wyandot people.

John and James Cissna had than enough evidence to convince them of the coming war. But they kept the information from their families lest they create a panic.

In a fall visit to the Wyandot village for trading, Chiefs Tarhe and Leather Lips had shown the Cissna brothers a sacred bundle of sticks left by Tecumseh.

With great care the chiefs explained Tecumseh's visit and the meaning of the single red stick in the sacred bundle. Although they religiously burned a piece every night, these two chiefs were not inclined to join in a war against the Americans.

When the great earthquake came, James and John both recognized its meaning.

The friendship of the Cissnas to these once ferocious people undoubtedly affected their choice to fight with American forces when war did break out. Most other Wyandot villages would fight with the British, but these two chiefs along Killbuck Creek remained with the Americans.

In the midst of the war, the two oldest Cissna brothers and John Burbank would find a peaceful people to settle among. They moved their families to what would become Holmes County, OH while the fighting was still going on.

The visit of the unnamed ancient warrior started three days of panic and debate. The inhabitants of River

Rouge gathered in groups both large and small to list options and dangers.

Some felt that their friendships with the natives had protected them in the past, and would again.

The more informed members reminded them that the war between France and England circled the globe on hundreds of fronts. In the past, they enjoyed peace with the natives only because of the British flag that flew over them.

After 1796, the community along River Rouge were no longer under English protection. They were fully under the American Flag.

If the U.S. were drawn into this conflict, the Michigan Territory would become a tender box that was a long way from governmental support.

In the end, the decision was clear if not unanimous.

Danger was eminent. Danger was close. Danger was clear. Caution was the best course.

Within a week, a large part of the River Rouge community was prepared for an exodus back to the closest secure position: the capital of Ohio at Chillicothe. It lay through 200 miles of forest trails. No road offered them assistance.

Excess food and animals were sold at Fort Detroit to the government purchaser who was buying up all supplies he could in anticipation of a war.

Precious belongings and children were packed onto horses and any beast that could carry a load.

Knowing that all of the main trails were being used by the Indians moving to join Tecumseh at Fort Malden, the party chose a less popular route. It required that no wagons make the trip. Everything would have to be carried on horses.

The Cissna men had been shown a trail which led through an unpopulated part of the Great Black Swamp. It avoided native towns. The only difficulty would be crossing the Maumee Miami River at a place where no ford was available.

Quickly felling two dozen trees, the men formed two rafts. These were used to portage the baggage, women, and children. The men swam across, as did every animal that could do so. On the other side of the river, the rafts were pulled into the brush, knocked apart and abandoned.

A refugee train left the River Rouge and arrived at Chillicothe the last week of April 1812. The six sons of Joseph Cissna -- John, James, Stephen, David, Joseph Jr., and Evans -- were greeted by their father's cousin, Stephen Cissna, Sr., who ran a tavern along the Scioto River.

Only Joseph Cissna, Sr.'s, daughter, Sarah, would remain to face the war in Detroit. Married to John Macomb, she worked tirelessly throughout the war to keep the Methodist Church alive and active in support of community needs. Her heroic efforts are recorded in the church's history as well as those of the city.

Tucked inside the fortified city itself, Sarah enjoyed much more protection than those who lived in the isolated farms.

A few weeks after their departure, most of the farmsteads on River Rouge were burned to the ground by Pottawatomie warriors who sought to avenge the loss of their traditional homelands.

The burning of abandoned houses had empty symbolism, and served little to quell the anger in their warrior hearts.

This was but one example of what was happening across the frontier of America that spring. The prudent were retreating from the wilderness to safer environments.

Everywhere, people stopped debating **if** war would come, and focused on **when** it would come.

The defeat at Tippecanoe had cost Tecumseh a great deal of momentum. Many warriors began to doubt his vision. Slowly he gathered a new army. But it was not large enough to wage war on the Americans alone.

He was forced to make an alliance with the British and fight under their leadership. Tecumseh's vision was dying and doomed to failure.

But hundreds of lives would be lost before the truth of that came clear to everyone.

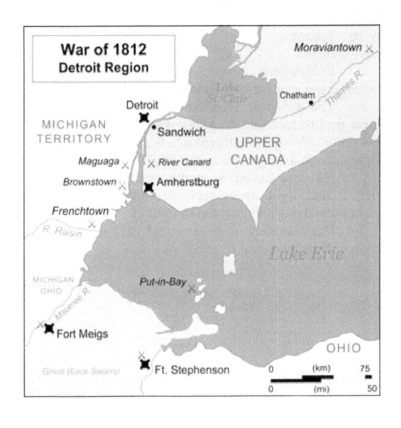

**War of 1812
Detroit Region**

Moraviantown

Lake
St. Clair

Chatham

Thames R.

Detroit

MICHIGAN
TERRITORY

Sandwich

UPPER
CANADA

Maguaga

River Canard

Brownstown

Amherstburg

Frenchtown

R. Raisin

MICHIGAN
OHIO

Maumee R.

Put-in-Bay

Lake Erie

Fort Meigs

Ft. Stephenson

OHIO

Great Black Swamp

| 0 | (km) | 75 |
| 0 | (mi) | 50 |

CHAPTER FOUR
Dayton, Ohio
April 25, 1812

"Do you intend to cower under your beds until Tecumseh and the Red Coats come and kill you in your sleep? We have one chance to act … and that is now! We licked them before; we can certainly do it again. Who is with me?"

Nicholas Cunningham had been standing on the porch of the hotel ranting for nearly 20 minutes. Finishing his speech, he stepped into the street and began to march up and down from one end of the block to another. A young lad with a drum began to accompany him. A crowd of nearly 500 men and women began to stir.

General Duncan McArthur himself had called this political rally. He had read orders from Washington War Department to raise an army of 700 militia men to protect Detroit and invade Canada if needed. Few doubted that it would be needed.

The day had gone like this: Following McArthur's speech, one man after another stepped forward to give an impassioned plea. Then, like Nicholas Cunningham, the speaker would step into the street and begin to march.

Those who were moved to volunteer, fell into ranks behind him. Cunningham would become the captain of the new company.

Those young volunteers had thus chosen Cunningham to be their captain. They marched up and down the street until the eighty men needed had volunteered. When the company was filled, loud cheering filled the streets.

Then another speaker stepped forward to raise his company. In this way an entire battalion was enlisted.

Political fervor reached a pitch. Men's hearts were stirred for war. They blushed with pride when the crowd cheered the formation of their company.

Among the men who stepped in behind Nicholas Cunningham was 18-year-old Stephen Cissna, Jr.

It was the words "Red Coats" that finally won him over.

His father, Stephen Cissna, Sr. had been one of the first Pennsylvania Riflemen to march to Boston in response to George Washington's call.

The emotions he felt when he heard details of fellow Americans being slaughtered in the woods were overpowering. Stephen Jr. just could not, not respond. He had to do something to save those innocent lives.

All his young life, Stephen Jr. had heard his father talk about the glory days of shooting and chasing Red Coats. The rifle which had helped win the Battle for Boston hung above the fireplace in his father's tavern in Chillicothe.

It was a trophy which had long inspired the boy's imagination. It had sparked many a heroic tale among those old soldiers who gathered to drink at his father's place.

Junior was given a few days between when he signed the enlistment and he when had to report for training. Stephen, Jr. made a beeline for his father's tavern. He found a great host of cousins had filled the tavern.

These were the refugees from Detroit. They had come hoping to find safety in face of the coming war.

The sight of his distressed relatives only served to fuel his desire to join the fight. His cousin William Cissna had been among the first casualties of this war. Now Junior would become the first Cissna to enter the war.

After a passionate and lengthy session of begging, the trophy/weapon was removed from its honored place. Stephen Cissna, Sr. passed the weapon to Stephen Cissna Jr. for him to use in the coming conflict.

"It drove the Red Coats from Boston; it should drive them from Canada too!"

With a torn heart, Stephen Cissna, Sr. watched his namesake march off to war.

He then realized he had only told the boy about the glory of his military service. He had failed to prepare him for the misery which accompanied it.

Doubt filled his mind in knowing he had raised the boy to be so eager to fight. His wife had more than a few words about how he had set his sons up for sacrificing themselves.

Cunningham's company organized at Dayton and immediately began training. Army life was a great thrill for the younger Stephen. Everything they did was given an air of importance. Even digging latrines seemed like a patriotic act.

At first, the shortage of equipment and lack of clear organization in the military structure seemed like minor inconveniences. They would grow to become the bane of every soldier's existence.

On May 10th, General William Hull arrived at Cincinnati and took command of 300 regular Army troops there. On May 25th, he arrived at Dayton and assumed command of three regiments of militia. The march to Detroit began immediately ... well, sort of.

The army was a chaotic mess. The commanders of the militia outranked the commander of the regular troops. Coordination was greatly hampered by this.

Many of the militia troops began to resent the junior officers elected in their company and mutinous attitudes were rampant.

William Hull was unable to focus his soldier's spirits for the task at hand. And the first task at hand was carving a 200-mile road from Urbana to Detroit.

They would do it in 20 days. It was needed to provide a ready supply route for military supplies and troops. Without it, Detroit had little chance of sustaining any British assault.

Stephen Cissna, Jr's first patriotic assignment was clearing trees and brush. Others would build the bridges and berms needed to keep the road open in rainy weather.

Unlike Cissna, many of his fellow soldiers had little experience or ability with firearms. He was in just as much danger from his fellows as he was from the enemy.

Ten days into the march, Pvt. Peter Vassar, one of the men in Col. MacArthur's regiment, was on guard duty. Daily the troops were given an allowance of whiskey. It was to purify the water and keep them from getting sick.

Vassar found little need to water down the whiskey and so his canteen held only "the good stuff." Having sipped a little too frequently, he decided to take a short nap under a shady tree.

Startled by a dream of an attacking Indian, he jerked awake, snatched up his rifle and shot the first thing he saw moving. Unfortunately, that turned out to be his fellow sentry, Private Joseph England.

Many such accidents had been happening among the untrained militia, but this was the first to prove fatal.

In an effort to set an example, General Hull ordered Vassar's ears to be cropped and had him paraded around the army with a sign saying "Tory" on his back. This was considered a punishment worse than firing squad.

Fifteen days into the march, life changed for Stephen Cissna, Jr. He was on axe duty that morning clearing away a small stand of birch which the engineer claimed blocked the proper path for the road to go.

He and his fellows were debating the engineer's wisdom about why the road could not go around the thicket.

Their rifles and cartridge boxes stood at rest no more than a few feet from each of the sweating men.

An axe swung. A log was shaken by the blow. A gun that had been resting upright slid sideways and discharged.

The ball passed through Stephen Jr's left arm, crippling it for the rest of his life. One report states that the rifle ball clipped the moustache of a Frenchman, passed through Cissna, and killed a third man.

Captain Cunningham would later write this description of the incident.

"The deposition of Capt. Nicholas Cunningham of lawful age and having been duly sworn, deposeth and saith that he commanded a company of Ohio volunteer militia under Col Duncan McArthur's regiment and under Brig General William Hull in July of 1812 in the War with Great Britain. This deponeth states that Stephen Cifsna was a private in his said company, and that in June 1812 the said Cifsna wilst on the line of his duty received a wound in the left arm by a T.N. Noyes (or Voyer), a private in Capt. Lucas' company. This deponent states as far as he can ascertain the afore said Stephen Sifsna received said wound without any provocation or fault, this deponeth states that the said Stephen Cifsna was carried by Mr. Bristoph to Detroit by General Hull on 16 August 1812, and was paroled by the enemy and returned to the state of Ohio. The deponent states that the said Stephen Cifsna was a faithful obedient soldier in all things appertaining to his duty."

When he examined Stephen, Jr. for a disability pension, Dr. Hayes made this description of the wound.

"The deposition of Doctor Adam Hays, a practicing Physician and Surgeon of the Town of Chillicothe, Ross County, and the State of Ohio. This deponent states that from an actual view of the wound and an examination of Stephen Cifsna under oath the following appears to be the true statement of this sayeth that he received a wound in June of 1812 in his left arm by a musket ball passing through the extensor muscles of said arm, dividing those muscles and he is thereby one half disabled from obtaining a subsistence by manual labor. A. Hayes M.D. 17 Sept 1816."

Stephen Jr. made the remainder of the march in the doctor's wagon. But it would be far from uneventful.

Arriving at the Maumee River, General Hull met Luther Chapin, captain of the Schooner *Cuyahoga*. Hull conceived what he thought would be a brilliant move. But it turned out to be disastrous for his cause.

On June 30th, Hull ordered that all unnecessary baggage and the 30 sick or wounded men and officers be placed aboard the schooner and sent ahead to Detroit. Captain Chapin moved regularly between these two ports and anticipated little trouble with making the journey.

Two unplanned events changed the course of events that day. General Hull had placed his drunkard son in charge of his personal baggage and files.

Being a man who constantly looked for the easiest way to do anything, Capt. Abraham Hull placed his father's personal papers and documents on the schooner without telling his father. He also sent along the Army's band, which he had grown tired of listening to.

The second event was precipitated by none other than John Jacob Astor himself. His American Fur Company was far better organized and capable of communication than the United States Government. He had already informed his agents that war had been declared on June 18.

General Hull had not received official notice of the declaration himself. But the agents of the American Fur Company and the Canadian Southwest Fur Company had informed the British commander at Fort Malden two days earlier.

In an expeditious haste, General Hull's army completed its road to Detroit. They expected to find the Schooner *Cuyahoga* waiting for them.

It was not.

Laying on the deck of the *Cuyahoga*, Stephen Cissna Jr. was enjoying his first good day since the accident. It was the first day that his pain was manageable. He could begin to move his fingers a little. He was now convinced that he would keep his arm.

The sun was shining brightly and the waters of the Detroit River were fairly mild. The wounded and sick men on deck were beginning to joke with each other.

Second Lieutenant George Gooding, who had been placed in charge of the wounded men, was beginning to feel optimistic. His wife had accompanied the army and was standing at his side watching the waters ahead of their vessel.

The calmer waters of the Detroit River were a welcome relief from the swells of Lake Erie.

Stephen Cissna was awed by the vastness of the lake. It seemed like an ocean to him. Returning to a river made him feel more at ease.

On July 2nd, the ship passed directly under the British guns of Fort Malden. Not one aboard the schooner was alarmed.

None knew that war had been declared two weeks earlier. None was alarmed at a large Indian canoe making its way across the lake towards them.

Provincial Marine Lieutenant Frederic Rolette stood at the front of the small boat. He was a professional soldier with five wounds and numerous battles behind him. Six seamen armed with cutlasses and pistols rowed the vessel.

Pulling close, Lt. Rolette ordered Captain Chapin to strike the sails and prepare to be boarded. Six British muskets were pointed at his chest. Chapin was speechless.

None on the vessel were aware what is happening until seven armed British soldiers stood in their midst on the deck. Though the Americans outnumbered the Brits five to one, none of the Americans had their weapons on deck with them. They were prisoners of war before they knew that they were officially at war!

Directing the *Cuyahoga* to the docks at Fort Malden, Lt. Rolette punctuated his triumph with an insult to the prisoners. At gunpoint, he demanded that the American band play "God Save The King" as the ship docked.

Stephen Cissna, Jr. watched in horror as his father's prized long rifle was seized along with the other American arms. He would never see the treasured weapon again, though he once thought he caught a glimpse of it in the hands of a savage.

Cissna's horror turned to terror when it came time to disembark the prisoners. Over 500 painted savages rushed the docks and formed a gauntlet. They intended to beat and further wound the prisoners as they passed through their ranks.

Lt. Col. St. George stepped forward to demand that the savages relent. To a chorus of blood-curdling screams, the prisoners were led through the crowd of Indians. It seemed that a massacre would erupt at any moment.

Just two of the prisoners had been led into the defile when one large brave leapt in front of them. A terrifying war cry exploded from his mouth as he raised a war club high in the air. The club never fell. The brave was only feigning a death blow.

The American fell to his knees in terror of immediate death. When he wet himself, the Indians erupted in howls and cheers. The threatening brave stepped back in line with a triumphant air.

St. George immediately turned the men around and pushed the prisoners along the dock and onto another ship, the *Thames*. He ordered his own men to begin throwing cargo from the *Cuyahoga* onto the docks and the warriors fell upon it as spoils of war. The American prisoners were temporarily forgotten by the horde. The *Thames* was ordered out into the channel and put to anchor.

It was now a prison ship.

Stephen's heart sank deep. For the first time in his young life, he thought that his death might be a welcome relief to the events he was enduring.

Among the baggage, General Hull's papers included detailed plans for invading Canada. All of the American plans approved by the President were now known by the enemy.

The one blessing is that being taken prisoner is the event which saved Stephen's life. He was able to receive the care of a qualified British Army doctor.

His infection was stemmed and his muscles set in the proper position to mend. His care by American medics had been sorely lacking.

From their floating prison, Stephen, Jr., and his fellow Americans could see the army of General Hull making its way along the river road. On two mornings, they could even hear the instruments calling the men to order.

To the prisoners, it was obvious that the American Army vastly outnumbered the forces they could see at Fort Malden and the tiny village of Amherstburg. They felt certain that Hull could take this place and rescue them without much trouble at all.

But their anticipated release never came. General Hull's campaign was a disaster. He was terrified of combat with the savages, and his fear caused him to be overly cautious to the point of inaction.

First, he decided he did not have enough food to feed his army.

He wrote the Governor of Ohio stating that he dared not proceed with attacking Canada until he had at least two months of supplies in the fort at Detroit.

Finally he invaded Canada with a force much larger than the British.

But Hull was terrified by the presence of Indians all around him. He refused to advance on any British town or fort, for fear of a massacre by the savages.

Duncan MacArthur and the other commanders clamored to attack Fort Malden, but Hull vacillated. Days, then weeks, went by without him advancing. Eventually he withdrew to Detroit without ever engaging the English.

Immediately, the British and their Indian allies launched a siege of Detroit. The delay had allowed reinforcements under General Brock to arrive from Lower Canada.

The siege ended with General Hull surrendering all his forces in the town, and in the field.

Actually, a fake letter by the British cowered Hull into surrendering.

The letter was written from the commander at Fort Malden to the commander at Fort Mackinac. It stated that the forces around Detroit were so strong that they only needed about 4,000 of the Indian warriors which Mackinac had planned to send them. The other 4,000 could wait until they were needed.

Unable to see the ruse, and imagining the forest full of thousands of wild savages, Hull collapsed.

He told himself and others that he had done so to prevent wholesale slaughter of every American in Michigan. Though he possessed a force much larger and better armed than his English counterparts, fear paralyzed Hull from action.

Hull would later be court martialed as a traitor for his actions at Detroit. That court sentenced him to be shot, but President Madison pardoned his life.

Suddenly faced with over a thousand American prisoners, and no way to provide for them, the English commander decided to parole the American soldiers.

The limiting condition of the parole was that they do not serve or fight in the current war until it ended, or until they were officially traded in exchange for English prisoners held by the Americans.

In August of 1812, Stephen Cissna, Jr. made a tearful and tragic return to his father's home in Chillicothe. Heaviest on his heart was the loss of his father's prized possession, "the rifle that won the Battle of Boston."

Heaviest on Stephen, Sr.'s heart was the way his beautiful son had been nearly destroyed by the wound he received. None of the glory of war returned to Chillicothe with these young men.

Stephen, Jr. married and had two sons. On 26 February 1814, he had recovered enough to marry the sweetheart of his youth, Sarah Finnemore King.

Stephen A. Cissna was born to them a year later on Feb 15, 1815. William Cissna followed with his birth on 17 June 1816. His sons, Stephen A., and William would become early settlers in Iroquois County Illinois. Cissna Park, IL bears its name in tribute to them.

In the fall of 1816, Stephen, Jr. was granted a Disability Pension from the Army for $4.11 per month. He died, however, in the little community of Clarksburg, Ohio on October 21, 1830. He was just 36 years old. His wounds from the war were stated as contributing factors to his death.

CHAPTER FIVE
Chillicothe, OH
26 June 1812

To men of Patriotism,
Courage & Enterprise.

EVERY able bodied man, from the age of 18 to 45 years, who shall be enlisted for the army of the United States, for the term of Five years, will be paid a bounty of SIXTEEN DOLLARS ; and whenever he shall have served the term for which he enlisted, and obtained, an honorable discharge stating that he had faithfully performed his duty whilst in service, he shall be allowed and paid, in addition to the aforesaid bounty, Three Months pay and One Hundred and Sixty Acres of Land , and in case he should be killed in action or die in the service, his heirs and representatives will be entitled to the said three months' pay and one hundred and sixty acres of Land to be designated, surveyed and laid off at the public expence.

Those who enlist for the term of 18 months shall be entitled to the same bounty, pay clothing and rations, the same provisions for wounds or disabilities, and to all other allowances (the bounty in land excepted) as above.

For the counties of Ross, Pickaway, Fayette and Athens, recruiting parties are stationed at Chillicothe, Circleville and Bainbridge, where the men " of Patriotism, Courage & Enterprise" may enlist themselves under the above flattering inducements offered by their country.

A L LANGHAM,
Captain of Infantry.

Recruiting Barracks,
Chillicothe, June 24, 1812.

Charles Cissna had noticed this flyer hanging on the front of every public building and several taverns he had passed on his way to visit his father. Here, on the front porch of his parent's tavern, he paused to read its message.

Charles was in a particularly bad mood that morning. Knowing that the Cissna tavern was a good place to drink, complain, and commiserate, he had decided to pay his old man a visit.

Over the years their relationship had been strained, and Charles was not very fond of his step-mother, Margaret. She had been nice enough in the beginning, but as her own children came on the scene, she had less patience for Stephen Cissna's older children.

Charles was having marriage problems ... again.

"Having a baby ain't so easy on a woman!" retorted his step-mother when he began to complain over a mug of Apple Jack. It was certain that he would not get much sympathy from that quarter.

"She has lost babies before, you know. It is a scary time for her," Margaret added to the argument before she disappeared back into the living section of the tavern.

Charles had not been aware he was having an argument until that moment.

Charles and Dorcus (Wilcutt) Cissna were one of those dynamic couples that build community. Each was intelligent and able to see the future clear enough to plan for it. They were equally matched in personal drive. And they each had a deep admiration for the other's abilities.

Two strong wills were drawn together in admiration and love. But those two strong wills were the factors that brought frequent tension to the union.

Much of their relationship was a contest of wills and opinions. The marriage was one of deep love and desire, but it often cycled between brief (yet intense) periods of desperate frustration. Once before, he had threatened to leave this marriage.

On Tuesday, 26 July 1808, when Dorcus was six months pregnant with his son, David, he had placed this ad in the paper: "Charles Cissna at Chillicothe offers all his household furniture for sale as well as his house and lots."

What made it so unusual a posting was that it was brief. Unlike similar advertisements, it did not mention any descriptions of the lots or furniture to be sold, nor information about how to contact the seller. It was more of a "personal ad" than a "classified ad."

Further, it does not appear the family was experiencing financial troubles. The following year, Charles and Dorcus purchased a prime town lot, #256, from John McDongal for $700.

Charles and Dorcus were very astute businesspeople, investing in real estate throughout Ross County. And they were among the first investors when the new town of Piketon was established further south.

But a clear message in the paper had been received by every man and woman in the county.

What kind of man sells his wife's furniture when she is six months pregnant? He did not end up selling any furniture or the house … or the town lots. But he had sent a message that put his wife on notice.

Charles Cissna could be a bit overdramatic at times.

If one asked his brother-in-law, John Fennimore, Charles could even be hot-tempered. At least that is what John told the court after an incident when he had been assaulted by Charles a few weeks before the marriage to Dorcus in 1801.

Court records show both Cissna and Fennimore were found guilty of assaulting each other, and fined $2. A short time later, Fennimore became Charles' brother-in-law.

But this day, the 26th of June 1812, Charles was in a troubled and restless mood.

"The Army" he thought. "Five years? She can't bother me there. Let her do things her way for a while. We are at war, so who could fault me?"

Leaving his parents' place in a huff, he walked purposefully to the two-story log building now being called "The Barracks." It had once housed the government of the North-West Territory.

Captain Angus Langham was waiting at a table just inside the door. After a few questions, Charles Cissna signed the enlistment. He was 29 years old.

Before the recruit could take the enlistment oath, administered by a civilian Justice of the Peace, he had to pass a medical examination. The Surgeon's Mate checked for ruptures, sore legs, scald heads, scurvy, "liability to fits," and habitual drunkenness.

Not too much attention was given to the qualification about "given to fits."

Charles was given just enough of the basic uniform to get him to the organization and training camp at Zanesville. And he was given three days to say goodbye to family before he had to report.

Charles Cissna became part of the 19th Infantry Regiment, newly created by Congress from residents in Ohio. He had promised to serve for five years, regardless of how long the war lasted.

America was at war.

Somehow the army must have seemed a more peaceful life than the one he knew with Dorcus and their four children.

The stop at Stephen Cissna's tavern had not done much to soothe his anger. His father was consumed with praise for Charles' half-brother, Stephen, Jr.

Junior had been among the first to sign up for the war. He was even now fighting somewhere near Detroit, possibly in Canada.

Charles' his step-mother always took Dorcus' part. So Charles Cissna found no sympathetic ears that day.

But things were settled now. He had made an oath to obey the President of the United States. For the next five years, the family (Dorcus) would just have to get along without him.

Charles tried excusing his action to his wife by claiming it was for financial reasons. He had received $16 in enlistment bonus, and he had also gotten three month's pay in advance -- another $18. He handed the $34 to her as some sort of penance.

"You are only going to make $6 a month. Farm laborers make $8 a month. We have help that we pay more than you are going to make!" she noted.

Dorcus was not the kind of woman who could be easily appeased by a pile of cash. Together they owned several lots and enterprises in the state capital of Chillicothe.

They were not in need of money. No matter how much she might complain about it.

If Charles had hoped for support from family and friends for his "patriotic" choice, he was disappointed.

Most people felt he was abandoning his family when they needed him most. His brother John was in a similar family situation and flat out told him it was a "stupid idea."

John would do his part for the war by hiring out as a teamster and private contractor to the army. He would be home to support his family far more than Charles. There were far easier ways to be patriotic.

Common opinion in that day was that a man needed to stay close to care for his wife and children. Charles Cissna was very much aware that his wife Dorcus could manage the family and their business enterprises without him.

In Charles' mind, what was not to like? Every day, a soldier received a ration of 1 ½ lbs. of beef or 2/3 lbs. of salted pork. He had never eaten so much meat before (nor would he ever again). In addition, he was given 1 pound of bread and 1 gill of whiskey or rum. Everything he needed was provided.

Twice each year he received a complete wardrobe of clothing and equipment. He had never dressed so well or looked so good in his life.

Congress was raising a new army. It would relieve the Army that General Hull had in Canada at the time.

When the worst happened, and Hull surrendered his army in August, the new Army became the only force defending the Northwestern Front.

Regiments were being raised in various states. The 19th Infantry was recruited in Ohio. The 17th

Infantry was recruited in Kentucky, the 16th from Pennsylvania, the 18th from South Carolina, and so on.

Each year every soldier was issued: 1 hat, 1 coat, 1 vest, 2 woolen overalls, 2 linen overalls, 4 pairs of shoes, 4 shirts, 2 pair of socks, 2 stockings, 1 blanket, 1 stock and clasp, 1 pair of gaiters, 1 linen frock, 1 linen pantaloon, 1 knapsack. The soldier also drew a .69-caliber iron-mounted Springfield musket, pattern of 1808, accoutrements, canteen, and haversack.

The soldier also received a small pocket-book to record every time he received at issue. When the company supply book was updated with a clothing issue, the soldier's book would also be updated. During company inspections, the soldier would provide his book to the 1st Sergeant who would compare what was issued with what the soldier then possessed.

And Charles learned the regimented life of a soldier.

He loved it!

Every day was carefully planned and scheduled to get the most benefit from it. Clothing and supplies had strict rules for storing and how they were worn. Every little detail was regulated. It was a very secure and structured life.

The best part was that you could complain about everything, and still appear patriotic and manly.

Even when you were in the field, every part of the army had its place. Below is a map of the traveling army camp. If you walked into any army camp, you knew exactly where to go to find the surgeon, or the quarter-master, or your own bed.

And private Cissna learned to fight the Army way. They marched in pretty lines to the fight. They stood shoulder to shoulder to face the enemy.

On command, they fired in unison. Their hands automatically reloaded in the fastest possible time without the soldier really thinking about it. His training did most of the thinking for him, allowing him to reload and shoot three times in a minute.

After three rapid volleys, they lunged forward in a ferocious bayonet charge. Most of the fighting was done in close quarters using blades of the bayonet, or the rifle butt as a club. It was a brutal business, and best attempted by trained men who fought in the coordinated fashion of soldier/brothers standing side by side in a phalanx.

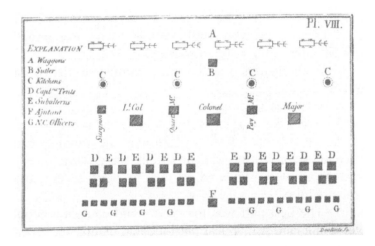

Firearms in his day did not have the power to reach out long distances and deal death with surgical precision. They were smooth-bore muskets with extremely poor accuracy. Even at just 300 feet, a .69-caliber lead ball's trajectory was dropping towards the ground.

Not much time was spent training the men to shoot straight, because the gun was not going to shoot where you aimed it anyway. The chorus of fire and lead was designed to shock the enemy.

Hopefully, it would soften their resolve and knock a few holes in their lines before you got there with the real weapon: your bayonet.

Most combat training was focused on how to skewer the opposition before they could skewer you. Practice consisted of jousting for hours on end. The idea was to train your muscles to instinctively know how to block and parry, and thrust or slash.

In today's American army this skill is still taught religiously, but with this admonition: "You should never let those *%* get close enough that you need to use this."

The 19th Infantry trained, equipped, and organized itself at Zanesville, Ohio. And within seven weeks of his arrival at Camp, Charles Cissna was marching into harm's way. Being older and more mature than most of the recruits, he was promoted to Corporal before their training had ended.

General William Henry Harrison, governor of Indiana, was given command of the Army of the Northwest. Second in command would be General James Winchester, who was responsible for the 19th Infantry.

The war did not wait long enough for them to become a fully trained fighting force.

By mid-august, General Winchester had marched the 19th Infantry to Vincennes, Indiana. From the territorial capitol, they would form the left flank of a re-invasion of Detroit and Canada.

The news of General Hull's surrender and the loss of 1,000 men was stunning to the entire nation.

The newly-raised regiments, including Charles Cissna, now realized how much was riding on their service.

Up and down the frontier the hubris of the Indians at Hull's surrender was inspiring terror. Settlers were being killed. Tribes were fighting together as never before.

William Henry Harrison was given command of the Army of the Northwest. He was ordered to retake Fort Detroit from the British and complete the plan to invade Canada from the west.

There was only one big problem. Actually, there were several thousand problems.

The forest between Vincennes and Detroit were full of raging war parties. Tecumseh had unleashed hundreds of small raiding parties to eradicate every American settler and trader in the Northwest territory.

These war parties carried the newest weapons that Great Britain had to offer them. They also had more ammunition than they could carry.

General Harrison knew that his army was badly outnumbered and outgunned. And his troops were as yet untrained in battle.

For the Army to charge directly towards Detroit would be a disaster.

Corporal Charles Cissna and most of the men in his regiment wondered why they were delaying.

Charles Cissna had family in Detroit. He had cousins who had fled from Detroit, and wanted to return. For Charles, retaking Detroit seemed like the most important task facing the army. And he felt ready to do that.

But General Harrison waited.

On 3 September 1812 two events marked the opening of wholesale combat in Indiana Territory.

The first disaster was when Kickapoo warriors attacked a small settlement at Pigeon Roost, about 100 miles south of present-day Indianapolis. It was a massacre of the goriest kind.

Word spread across the Northwest Territory like wildfire. A general panic set in among the settlers.

It was now obvious that this was not just a war between armies at far away forts.

With the battle for Detroit won, the natives took a new direction. Spreading across the forests they intended to bring death to every white family they met.

This was no longer a war of official combatants.

It was actually two wars. For the British it was a war for territory, fought by regular Army Officers. For Tecumseh and his warriors, this was a war of terror and extermination.

Isolated farmers in northern Indiana and Ohio began to follow the example of those who had lived around Detroit. Fleeing before the murderous onslaught, they raced their families to the safety of bigger towns in the south.

Charles Cissna's hometown of Chillicothe, Ohio was soon overcrowded with refuges. The letters from home were alarming. But there was no way he could leave his post and return to help.

The same day, that Pigeon Roost was destroyed, a large party of Kickapoo, Miami, Pottawatomie, Shawnee, and Winnebago warriors left Prophet's Town and laid siege to Fort Harrison along the Wabash River.

When he marched to attack Prophet's Town in 1811, General Harrison had built a series of stockades to hold supplies. These were small forts, holding supplies, and guarded by only small detachment of soldiers. They were very vulnerable

Where modern day Terre Haut now stands, the army had constructed a small stockade on top of a bluff with a commanding view of the river. It had been named after General Harrison.

As Tecumseh's army headed south, flooding the forests along the Wabash River with dozens of war parties, Fort Harrison was their first target.

The fort was defended by a force of sixty officers and men under the Command of Captain Zacchary Taylor (who would later become President Taylor).

Tecumseh himself was said to be at the head of this force, and it was only with great tenacity and heroism that Fort Harrison survived long enough to be relieved.

When a runner brought news that Fort Harrison was under siege, the 19th Infantry (including Cpl. Charles Cissna) was immediately dispatched to go to their aid.

It was a 70 mile trek through the forest from Vincennes to Terre Haut. A crude wagon trail had been built a year earlier. It was now overgrown and there was no longer a real road.

The Army had to march through the forests in three parallel lines.

Supplies and the bulk of the force were kept in the center. On each flank, a row of soldiers provided a first line of defense should they be attacked from the side.

Charles Cissna's company was assigned to protect the left flank. They were to march as close to the Wabash River as possible. This enabled them to guard against war parties in canoes.

If they came under attack, there was the promise that soldiers in the middle file would quickly come to their rescue.

The 19th Infantry received its baptism of fire on that rushed march to relieve Fort Harrison.

There was no large scale battle. The natives staged harassing attacks in small groups as the army moved toward relief of the fort. The soldiers never knew where or when they might come under fire.

And just as quickly as they started the fight, the natives would disappear back into the forest and be gone. Sometimes, they left so quick that the soldiers could find nothing to shoot back at.

The terrain was very rough.

At a point where a deep creek merged with the river, the main body drifted far to the right. They men in the left column could no longer see their fellow soldiers through the woods.

This spot had been chosen carefully as an ambush.

Climbing down the bank to wade across the creek, Charles heard the first shot. It was instantly followed by a dozen more. A wave of terrifying war cries swept over them.

Even though they had been marching under full alert, looking for any signs of the enemy, they were taken by surprise.

Men began to fall and cry out in pain. There were injured men both in front of and behind Corporal Cissna. It was mass confusion while the officers sorted out what was happening. They could not tell how many of the enemy there might be.

The soldiers began to pull together in small groups. This broke the line of the column and the men were now fighting in an uncoordinated way.

This was a disastrous response to an ambush. But with the soldiers so widely scattered, there was no way to organize an effective counterattack.

Cpl. Charles Cissna had just stepped down a steep embankment into the creek bed when the shooting started. There were three other men also in the creek bed when the attack began. Being in the sunken place had protected them from the first volley.

In just a few moments, four other soldiers came tumbling into the creek to join them. Two had come running from the south, and two had come from the north. The two from the north were carrying the sergeant. Though he struggled to hold his pain, it was obvious that this wound was catastrophic.

This left Cpl. Cissna in charge. It seemed certain that they were going to be overrun. Their worst fear was being in hand to hand combat with a tomahawk wielding savage.

From both directions along the riverbank, Charles Cissna could hear men scream as they were being struck down. The entire company was sure to perish if something was not done quickly.

Leaving one man to watch over the sergeant, Charles ordered the others to reload and follow him.

Wading up the creek, with the high bank to cover them, Cpl. Cissna led his men about 50 yards upstream. Then at his command, they popped up from their hiding place and fired at the enemy. Half of them fired to the right, and half to the left.

The native warriors had been hiding behind trees as they conducted the ambush. When it was certain they had killed enough of the soldiers, they planned to run among them and finish the job with tomahawks.

But Charles Cissna had a surprise for them. They were now being fired at from the side. They had been flanked by the Americans sneaking up the creek.

Suddenly, the advantage of surprise was completely lost. The warriors were being fired at from the men along the river. But trees gave them protection.

Now they were being shot at from the side. No trees would protect them. They had lost their protection.

But the biggest danger was behind them.

The main army was several hundred yards east. When they heard the firing, they would certainly charge forward to help their fellow soldiers. But it would take them several minutes to organize and respond.

The Indian army had counted on being able to attack swiftly, do as much damage as possible. Then they would slip away before the main body of the army could attack their rear.

Every man in feathers and buckskin knew their time was up. As one, they abandoned the fight running north and south to escape the ranks of soldiers closing in on them.

The ambush was over.

His actions during his first combat experience would get Charles Cissna promoted to Sergeant.

Infantry marched on to relieve Fort Harrison. But the native army was not about to relent without a vicious fight.

The 19th Infantry had to battle its way through the thousands of Indians scattered through the forests surrounding the fort. This was a guerilla war. The enemy sprang ambush after ambush, suddenly appearing from behind trees and rocks.

Charles Cissna and his fellow soldiers had not been trained for this kind of fighting. You could not find someone to shoot at until he suddenly appeared ready to shoot you.

Approaching the fort was a slow and deadly process. But the 19th Infantry persisted. They learned how to fight Indian style in the days of approaching Fort Harrison.

Sgt. Cissna had learned that the best response to an ambush was a flanking maneuver.

They arrived in time to save the beleaguered garrison. And in a fierce battle that followed, the natives were driven from the field.

This was the first American victory on land during the war. Praise was given to his entire regiment. Charles Cissna was promoted to Sergeant in a ceremony which was intended to boost moral of an army which had been badly bloodied.

Two days later, on September 5th, Tecumseh directed an army of about six hundred warriors from the Ottawa Nations to infiltrate and attack the American garrison a Fort Wayne.

This was the point where the Maumee, St. Joseph and St. Mary's Rivers come together. It was a major crossroads for traveling by river from the Ohio and Mississippi up to Lake Erie.

Again, the soldiers manning the fort were able to resist. But their survival was in great doubt.

General William Henry Harrison ordered his new army to launch an offensive in defense of Fort Wayne. It was 200 miles from Fort Harrison to the beleaguered fortress.

That would be 200 miles of walking through virgin forests. Sgt. Cissna and his men were on guard every step of the way. Attack could come from any direction at any time. It was a slow march. Every step forward was made cautiously.

General Harrison decided he would use this march to break the resolve of the warriors who had rallied to Tecumseh. He would destroy every Indian town within his path.

The Americans destroyed their homes, their families, and their winter food supply. They hoped this might make some of the warriors abandon Tecumseh's army and go home to protect their families.

The 19th Infantry and other regiments were ordered spread into the woods of northern Indiana as they marched towards Fort Wayne.

Their assignment was to locate and burn every Indian town they could find. The enemy was to be engaged at every opportunity.

Charles Cissna was appalled with the brutality he saw among his fellow soldiers. Many of them had lost family members to the rage of the Indians. This was their chance to unleash their anger.

Their revenge on the red man was severe. Little effort was made to distinguish combative tribesmen from those who had chosen to remain neutral.

Harrison strengthened the garrison at every small fort across Indiana, packing their storehouses with massive amounts of supplies needed for the coming conflict.

On November 17th, 19th, and 20th regiments charged into Prophet's Town and burned it to the ground. Following orders from Tecumseh, the warriors had withdrawn and the town was empty.

But Charles Cissna and his brothers-at-arms were stunned to find the stockpile of weapons and food. All of it carried the markings of English military stores. It was obvious that the Indian Army had enough weapons and food to continue this war for several years.

At least they had had that much until the American's burned it at Prophet's Town.

On December 17th, the army approached the Delaware and Miami villages where the Mississinewa River joins the Wabash River near present-day Marion, Indiana. Resistance to the Americans was fierce and a two-day battle cost many lives.

At this point Sgt. Charles Cissna had become battle hardened. He was not six months into his army career. But in his heart he carried a firm hatred of the Indians and British.

In the twentieth century, a term "gung ho" was coined to describe a soldier who had fully committed himself to the struggle before them. That term describes the transformation which Charles had undergone.

He was now totally committed to the prosecution of this war. He held nothing back. His commanders saw him as the consummate soldier and offered him increased responsibility.

When they had relieved Fort Wayne of the native army surrounding it, General Harrison changed his strategy. It was now noticeably clear that his army was badly outnumbered, and out supplied.

It was 300 miles back to his supply depot at Vincennes. Harrison knew he was not ready to attack Detroit.

General William Henry Harrison left another part of his army to strengthen Fort Wayne. His army was getting smaller with every detachment he left behind to protect a string of forts.

What remained of the Army of the Northwest, marched up the Maumee River. At a place now known as Perrysburg, OH the men constructed a large fort. It was named Fort Meigs to honor the govern or of Ohio.

This was to be the new base of operations for Harrison's army. The men were allowed to rest as they waited for more regiments and built a large stockpile of supplies. During the next few months, Sgt. Charles Cissna was responsible for keeping men on guard duty. Sometimes he led scouting missions into the forest.

The Winter months were demanding but quieter than he had known throughout the Fall.

CHAPTER SIX
Chillicothe, Ohio
10 July 1812

"You had better come quick! I think Junior is in trouble."

Margaret Cissna had never seemed so desperate. Exploding through the front door of their tavern it was clear that everyone in the room needed to come with her, that very instant.

"What do you mean?" asked her husband.

"The governor said that the army in Detroit is in trouble. He is going to make a speech in a few minutes."

Stephen Cissna, Sr. and the five old men sitting in the tavern instantly came to their feet and hurried across the street to where the Ohio Governor J. Meigs kept his office. A crowd of 300 had already gathered, and more were streaming in from every direction.

This was how news was disseminated in the State Capital of Ohio. Frequently, the Governor himself would simply step into the street and announce urgent information directly to the people.

Those who were not in town at the moment, would have to read about it in the *Scioto Gazette* the next day.

With the country having been at war for a month, and many of Ohio's sons serving in the militia under General Hull, this was destined to be an important announcement.

At 8:30 a.m., Governor Meigs stepped into the sun-drenched porch and came quickly to the point.

General Hull had invaded Canada. But he was stalled from progress for lack of supplies. In a personal letter to the Governor, General Hull stated he needed at least two months' supplies as quickly as possible or the entire fate of his army would be in doubt.

Meigs went on to say that these supplies were in fact already purchased and ready for shipment. But there was no one who could take the badly-needed food to the army at Detroit. He had a plan, but needed help.

At the governor's side was well dressed man. He now stepped forward. Standing in front of the crowd was a young lawyer named Henry Brush.

"Young Brush here has family in Detroit. He has volunteered to organize and lead a company of militia to escort the supplies to the Army. I am asking for volunteers to form this company with Brush as its captain. Who will join him?"

The governor fairly pushed Henry Brush into the street and he began to march to the end of the block. Young men jumped into formation behind him. By the time, he had made it from one end of the block to the other, he had 100 men behind him.

Stephen and Margaret Cissna both grew pale.

Among the ranks following the new Captain Henry Brush were their sons, Joseph and James. Two sons of the old man's cousin, Cpt. Joseph Cissna, were also in the ranks, Stephen P., and Joseph Jr. Joe Junior was chosen to serve as a corporal in the third platoon, under Lt. Entreken.

Four more Cissna men were going to the war! And as of that moment, they had still heard nothing of the fate of Stephen Cissna, Jr.

Margaret grabbed her stepsons and pulled them to the edge of the crowd. In hurried words, she tried to get them to reconsider.

Both boys had the same response. "Someone has to go. If not us, who?"

Map of Chillicothe Ohio during War of 1812

Cissna Tavern & Store

Stephen Cissna owned a tavern at lot 277, a store at 276, 149.
Charles Cissna, son of Stephen owned Lots 258, 256, 220, 176, and 159
Stephen Cissna, Jr owned a house at lot 149.
John Cissna, son of Stephen, owned lots 227 and 35.
William Cissna, son of Stephen operated a business at lot 276
Samuel Cissna, a nephew/cousin of Stephen Cissna owned lot 223, and operated a tailor shop and haberdashery at lot 277 in which he partnered with Charles Cissna.

The young men were led to the two-story log building which had once housed the territorial government. Upon signing the enlistment, they were divided into three platoons and training began immediately. They would march at first light the next morning.

People in the crowd began to shout, "They don't have any uniforms."

"How will they fight without equipment?"

While the Governor had received food and ammunition by boat, he did not have equipment to outfit any new military units.

Patriots step forward. Ideas were shouted out. They would be seized and acted upon without debate.

Time was critical. No one had ever seen a town of people work together so quickly.

A group of ladies said that the men needed uniforms. After a quick debate, white one-size-fits-all hunting shirts were chosen. Someone began to collect money and the material was purchased within an hour.

Sixty women began to hand sew the shirts. By sundown that day, 108 men had been provided matching white shirts.

A group of men announced that they would create canteens and cartridge boxes for them. Of course, these needed a shoulder strap to complete them. This same group of men vowed to produce the needed equipment in one day.

Leather was fairly scarce and difficult to work with. This proved problematic. Most all available leather was already being made into something else.

The town's people succeeded only by cannibalizing harnesses, belts, and any leather items which could be spared.

A group of former soldiers observed that the men needed ammunition. These were the same men who liked to frequent the Chillicothe taverns and relive their adventures. Two taverns were immediately converted to munitions factories.

The inn of Stephen and Margaret Cissna was one of these.

Veterans of the revolution insisted that each cartridge contain a ball and three small shots. This provided the greatest killing power for combat munitions.

By the end of the day, 2,000 rounds of munitions were carefully measured, wrapped tightly in paper cartridges, and filled the new cartridge boxes.

Twenty rounds per cartridge box. One box per man.

In less than twenty-four hours, a company of 100 men had been recruited, taught to march and the basics of military discipline, and were now fully equipped for battle.

It was an amazing thing to see. All of the cost was born by the citizens themselves, either in donations of cash, labor, or materials.

The people of Chillicothe had something to prove. In 1810, the state legislature had moved the capital to Zanesville. Only a few months before this day it had been moved back to Chillicothe.

Loss of the capital meant a loss of the cash flow which comes along with it.

So, the people of Chillicothe were motivated both by patriotism, and by the desire to prove to the Governor that their town was by far the best place for his office to be.

Their response was impressive in its generosity and its effectiveness.

While the town was abuzz with preparations, the two-story log government building was equally active. The soldiers had to be screened before they enlisted, and then hastily trained.

Examinations were cursory but important. Old Dr. McAdow pretty much knew all the young men in the company, having treated a suitable number of them. He knew most by name, and already knew if they were fit to serve or not.

Because each volunteer was required to furnish his own equipment, this had to be inspected as well. A local cobbler was asked to be sure that every man accepted for duty had adequate shoes for 1,000 miles of travel. If they had no shoes, they were turned away.

Two gunsmiths inspected each soldier's personal weapon to be sure it was service worthy. Some of the men showed up with guns that had not been fired in 10 years.

Sergeants inspected the bedrolls. These were nothing more than the blankets they slept with every night at home. Inside each was an assortment of items they thought they might need. The Sergeant quickly discarded those things which provided more weight than utility.

In this regard the four Cissna cousins had a distinct advantage. Their fathers had served in some of the harshest fighting in the Revolutionary War. They had heard many lectures about what a man needed to survive.

The Sergeants then conducted classes in military conduct. They were taught to stand at attention and salute. They were taught things which seemed simple and obvious, but which the men could not seem to grasp without a lot of screaming and threatening.

By noon, they were all brought out into the hot sun and taught to march. Some of them complained that they already knew how to walk.

"That's the way your mommas taught you!" screamed the sergeant. "Now you will learn the Army way!".

Then they learned to run in formation. Then they learned to swing in flanks and wheel around in directions commanded by the change in drum rhythm.

To be honest, the old veterans of the town thought they looked a sorry mess.

"Don't worry," said Stephen Cissna Sr. "they will learn quick. We did!"

This unit had one thing going for it that most of the units in General Hull's army did not have. These were lads who were all from the same town. They knew each other well.

Old rivalries were set aside as they adopted a central purpose. They worked together. They helped each other. They encouraged each other.

A few of the men were like the sons of Joseph Cissna. They had just arrived in Chillicothe as refugees from Detroit. They felt the same unity. And now that their families were safe, they were eager to get back to protect their homes.

Captain Brush called his lieutenants together on the second floor of the log building. He needed maps and information. The rider who had brought the letter from General Hull helped them complete a rough map of the newly-built road.

It would provide a quick journey, provided there were no surprises from the enemy. The officers knew that their enemy thrived on surprises.

Ensign William Hurt and Corporal Joseph Cissna were among the men who had just come from Detroit. Coming from a family of *voyageurs*, Cissna helped fill in information about Indian towns and war trails that were frequently used.

The men from the River Rouge settlement provided a great deal of intelligence in the planning.

Their knowledge would prove invaluable throughout the journey.

Henry Brush was discouraged to learn details about the Great Black Swamp which lay between them and Michigan. If they could stay on the new road it should not be a problem.

However, the Great Black Swamp posed more problems than just travel. It was thick with mosquitos at this time of year. Endemic malaria was a constant threat to travels there.

In fact, a sizable number of General Hull's men had contracted it as they built the road.

The Black Swamp was 25 miles wide and about 90 miles in length from East to West. Much of it was simply impassible by wheeled vehicles.

Joseph Cissna and William Hurt carefully explained to Brush that there was only one way to cross it: during the day, and in a rush.

They would need to camp just above the swamp at Fort Findley. And the 30 miles to Fort Miami would need to be covered in one day. It would be foolish to try and camp their supply train in the midst of the swamp.

"Some missionaries tried to camp in the swamp one night," related Joseph Cissna Jr. "On Sunday morning, they woke to find that every man, woman, child, and critter in their party was 10 pounds lighter than when they went to bed on Saturday night. That is how hungry them skeeters are."

Henry Brush had lots of things to worry about. He had never commanded a company of men. His sole authority came from being a respected lawyer.

This would not be an easy assignment. Taking green soldiers into the midst of a land teaming with savages and swamps; driving stubborn cattle and pack animals through wilderness roads; and most troubling of all … how could he convince these men that he knew what he was doing?

At dawn on July 21st Captain Brush and a company which included four young Cissna men marched to Urbana. Without hesitation, they loaded the supplies from the wagons onto horses and mules. They began to march up the road built by General Hull a year earlier.

Private Stephen P. Cissna and his brother Corporal Joseph Cissna, Jr. proved themselves invaluable on the trip to Detroit. Both had been raised in the back woods. Each knew how to communicate with the lone Indians they encountered along the way.

And having worked for their older brothers as *voyageurs*, they understood some basic rules for traveling with a large group through the forest.

"Don't pee in the stream! Someone downstream may be trying to fill his canteen."

"Pack your bedroll tight the first time and you won't have to stop and repack it during the day."

"Keep the campfire smokey. It keeps the skeeters away. And be sure you smoke your blanket and clothes before you go to bed."

"Squaw's Mint (Pennyroyal) will keep the bugs and skeeters off you when you have guard duty at night."

Stephen P. Cissna was particularly adept at knowing which plants were helpful or edible. He had a knack for remembering such things.

Even when traveling with his brothers, Stephen P. was far more concerned with learning the basic rules of camp hygiene than he was the ways of the forest. He often was busy taking care of the community meals and other needs.

Stephen P. Cissna was fascinated by the cause and effect of trivial things. And he loved to find a better way to do things whether that was how to prepare the ground to sleep on, or how to hang food in the trees.

Sixty horses and mules were loaded with 200 to 300 pounds of supplies each. They had to be carefully unloaded and cared for each night.

Army policy was that the health of the animals was more important than the health of the men. So, great attention was paid to each beast.

In the morning, each beast must be inspected, saddled with a pack frame, and their load very carefully tied to the frame. The weight must be balanced so as to not tax the beast too greatly. The lashings must be tight enough to not allow shifting.

It required a great deal of attention to detail, and it was never accomplished without very loud advice screamed by the Sergeants and Corporals.

The fifty beef critters were another matter altogether. They had not been trained to work closely with humans. They were driven, not led. They tended to wander off.

Cattle have their own set of rules which a drover has to understand.

Having been penned together for several weeks, these creatures now had established their own community. It was simple and even obvious if you took the time to watch them.

Each steer and cow knew his or her place in the herd. When the herd moved, their rank determined their place in the line. If you pushed one beast to get in line at the wrong place, the entire group became unsettled and balked.

To succeed in pushing the herd forward, required letting them choose whom they would walk behind and next to.

You had to let them choose which beast was going to lead the herd down the path you chose. Sometimes you had to trick that beast into thinking he had chosen the path himself.

Corporal Cissna thought they were a lot more like people than anyone gave them credit for.

Without wagons, the train would move much quicker, covering 15-25 miles a day instead of 10. The newly-constructed military road allowed for easier travel and in two weeks they were at the River Raisin.

At the Raisin, they were just three day's march from Detroit.

Here things began to fall apart.

Here they would leave the shelter of the forest and follow the river road. They would be easily visible and within cannon shot of the British at Fort Malden just across the Detroit River.

Capt. Henry Brush had guessed that the British would do anything to keep him from delivering his cargo. The Americans, the Indians, and the British all could benefit from the wealth of food and supplies he was bringing to Detroit.

He had anticipated little trouble getting this far. And very little had appeared. Most of the warriors were surrounding Detroit, not watching the roads to the south.

But Brush knew he was in trouble now.

The men from the River Rouge community now became vitally important to the campaign. Knowing this area well, they were sent out as scouts to see what lay ahead.

General Hull was waiting on the Canadian side of the Detroit River.

Terrified of the thousands of Indians he was certain surrounded him, General Hull was afraid to move in any direction. He needed to retreat.

But he wanted to know his supplies were safe in Fort Detroit before he returned to it. At least that is what he told his staff.

But his officers and men were beginning to see that he was paralyzed with fear of the savage warriors around him.

Tecumseh and General Brock decided that the supply train would make a very tempting bait to get the Americans to divide their forces.

So, Indian patrols were sent to fill the woods around Capt. Brush's men.

They never made a direct attack, but isolated men were assaulted. Several times the men would find arrows sticking in the sides of the cattle or protruding from the packs.

Captain Brush was effectively penned down. He had placed his men in a good defensive position. But he could advance no further without risking lives and cargo.

Now began two weeks of sheer hell for the men of Brush's command.

They dared not let their guard down either day or night. The animals were herded into a tight space and hobbled. Half of the men stood watch for 4 hours while the other half slept.

There was no down time. Their lives cycled between hyper alert and exhausted sleep. No fires could be built at night because the light made your silhouette an easy target for creeping Indians.

Every night there were attempts by the savages to steal animals, equipment, or hair. Every day, a group of savages tested the perimeter of their defenses.

Food was cold, until the day when the savages had mortally wounded one of the beeves. In desperation, it was slaughtered and cooked in large chunks over a roaring fire. It would be the only hot meal the men had as they waited along the River Raisin.

Corporal James McDougal, another of the River Rouge men, was chosen to take a message to Hull.

"We dare not advance further with the few men I have. Please send an escort that we might bring the goods safely to the fort."

Hull immediately dispatched a unit to bring his needed supplies into safety.

The trap was set.

August 5, 1812
Wyandot village of Manuaga

The village had been abandoned.

Just a few miles from the American fort at Detroit, its inhabitants have moved en-masse across the Detroit River to be with Tecumseh and the British Army.

General Hull had ordered Major Thomas Van Horne to leave the American camp in Canada and rescue Capt. Brush's supply train. On the way, he was to pick up a force of 200 militiamen, waiting on the American side of the river.

This was the same group of stubborn men who refused to cross into Canada with Hull. Their argument was that militia had no constitutional authority to fight on foreign soil. So, they had been left behind.

Van Horne's soldiers cautiously approached the River aux Ecorse. At dawn, they stealthily entered Managua.

The ghostliness of the abandoned town had an ominous feel. The men from Kentucky were extremely on edge.

Just beyond the town, the road forked around a corn field.

Without hesitation, or discretion, the force divided and followed each fork.

When the two groups of 100 soldiers each could no longer see each other, Tecumseh sprang his trap on the left column.

On the right, Robert Lucas and his men were unable to reach their companions before the damage was done. Three corpses lay dead in the road.

The men were badly shaken and the rear guard was in panic. But just as quickly as they appeared, the Indians vanished into the tall corn.

Their confidence quickly fading, the militia men were ordered to press on toward Brownstown. Along the way, several of the French settlers came out and warned them an even larger Indian force was waiting for them at that place.

But the Americans did not trust the French. Many of the French settlers were pro-British and had provided false reports in the past.

On guard, moving in triple file with mounted men between the outer flanks, the detail slowly proceeded to their waiting fate.

At Brownstown Creek, the road narrowed to a small ford. Beside it grew thick bushes along both sides of the road. Across the ford was a large corn field in full height. It is a perfect place for an ambush.

Tecumseh was waiting with twenty-four Shawnee and Ottawa and one white man. Alexander Elliott was the son of Matthew Elliott, a man whose name every American recognized as a traitor during the revolution.

The odds were twenty to one in favor of the Americans. But the attack came so swiftly, and the cries of the savages were so disheartening, that Van Horne believed he was outnumbered.

As he turned to order retreat he saw that most of his soldiers had already thrown their weapons away and started to run back up the road.

Van Horne lost eighteen men killed and twenty wounded. Seven of the dead were officers. Some seventy men were missing when the unit straggled back to Fort Detroit.

Many were hiding, every man for himself, in the forest. Slowly the survivors trickled back to the fort over the next few days.

One young militia man had been taken captive by the Indians. As they debated his fate, Pottawatomie warriors carried in the body of Blue Jacket. The highly-esteemed warrior was the only casualty among Tecumseh's men.

In retaliation for Blue Jacket's death, the man was cruelly hacked and stabbed to death by the women who accompanied the warriors. It was a horrible death, and designed to be intensely humiliating.

General William Hull was mortified at the news.

He was now convinced that he was badly outnumbered. Hull sent word back to Ohio that he needed another 2,000 men if he were to complete the task at hand. Then he ordered his men to withdraw to the safety of Fort Detroit.

His plans to invade Canada ended without engaging the enemy in even one serious challenge.

Captain Brush greeted the news with a somber look. His situation was now clear. The Indians had not attacked him because they were using him for bait.

Any force that Hull sent to rescue him would be met with ambush. Eventually, the Indians would decide to just fall on him and claim his baggage as prize.

Brush realized that he could not complete his mission without great loss of life.

The officers and men began to weigh alternatives. These were not trained soldiers which Captain Brush was leading. They were volunteers without any experience in fighting.

Retreat into the safety of Ohio seemed the best option. But how should they do that? If they returned on the same road, they would be easy prey for any pursuing force.

Now the men of River Rouge provided the intelligence which would save their lives. There was another route through the Great Swamp; it had been taken by the River Rouge refugees just two months earlier.

They had chosen it because it avoided any Indian towns or major trails. They chose it because it was shorter and held only one large obstacle.

It required that they cross the Maumee River at one of its deepest and swiftest places.

Corporal Cissna and Ensign Hurt explained that they had accomplished it by building two small rafts and pulling the baggage across with ropes.

Joseph Cissna pointed out that the logs used for the rafts were still lying in the brush where they had been abandoned. With an hour's work, they could become rafts once again.

Captain Brush agreed it was their best option, but waited to see what General Hull would do next. The general's response would surely be dramatic.

August 9, 1812
Village of Manauga

Hull sent another relief force to bring the supply train into Detroit. This time it was a force of 600 men, 200 of which are regular army troops and not likely to run at the first blush of warfare. They were supported by cavalry and canon.

General Hull had every intention of succeeding this time. This force expected to make it all the way to Brownstown before they were attacked, but they were wrong.

This time, Tecumseh had a larger force of natives, and he was joined by a large force of British regulars and militia. They laid the trap just before the Americans would enter the abandoned Indian village.

Battle began in a flurry of Indian assaults. The natives were on one side and British were on the other. Confusion quickly clouded the battle.

The Americans fought bravely. The cannons were brought into play, but the cavalry failed to respond to the commands they were given.

Tecumseh had coordinated the attack to be brief and vicious. First the Indians assailed the flank nearest them. They withdrew. And then the British hit the other side.

Considerable damage was done to the Americans. Tecumseh attacked again, and the British used the distraction to retreat to their boats and cross back over the Detroit River.

Now Tecumseh had his warriors retreat as well.

It was a classic one-two-three punch.

The Indians continue to slowly fall back into the forest, devouring any American who pursued them. Most Americans threw their back packs away in order to run and fight. This move proved disastrous.

The sun faded early. It was not going behind the horizon but behind a strong line of thunderstorms moving in from the west. Soon a blinding downpour began which would last until just before dawn.

Caught in the woods without shelter, the Americans were scattered and helpless to the elements. The morning came to find no enemy in sight but a badly mangled army scattered pitifully throughout the forest.

The relief column was recalled to Fort Detroit on August 11th.

The Americans had lost 18 men killed and some 60 wounded. But few of the remaining soldiers had their equipment.

The British had lost 6 killed and 21 wounded.

General Hull declared the battle to be an American victory.

But Captain Brush's supply train was still marooned on the banks of the River Raisin.

News of the battle troubled Brush greatly and he ordered his men to keep all of the animals loaded and ready to move at a moment's notice.

They could not keep up this state of readiness for very long. Brush had to decide soon.

His scouts told him that he was still surrounded by Indians. But most of those had been called away to fight in the ambushes.

Tecumseh though that Brush's command were stranded and would not be going anywhere. He pulled many of the warriors back for other fighting.

The enemy surrounding him no longer had numbers enough to attack him with effectiveness.

Brush had a strong defensive position.

Since the killing was taking place elsewhere, many of the warriors around them had grown tired of waiting.

The River Rouge men were tired of waiting as well. They were extremely aware of how powerful the natives could be in these woods.

They suggested to Brush that there was an alternate route to Detroit which could not be seen by the British at Amherstburg. Though twice as long and far more difficult than the river road, it was doable if they had enough help.

General Hull made his last attempt to rescue the supplies. Colonels Lewis Cass and Duncan McArthur were each given 350 men and ordered to secure the alternate route.

It made a long loop far to the west; circumventing all of the settlements. They marched in loud display from Fort Detroit at noon on August 14th.

Captain Brush's men had now been waiting for three weeks. For three weeks these men had been cowering behind log barricades expecting a full assault by the Indians. It had been 20 sleepless and nerve racking days.

The American force of General Hull was more than 2,000 strong. The British force under General Brock was only about 1,300. Most of those were native warriors.

Though the British general was outnumbered, he had what Hull did not have. He had a willingness to gamble.

Brock sent his forces across the river to launch a siege on Fort Detroit.

General Hull's men intercepted a British messenger with a fake message to Fort Mackinac. It stated that the English had a vastly superior force and that another 4,000 Indians would soon arrive here from Mackinac. William Hull was stricken with panic.

Without putting up a fight, Hull negotiated surrender to the British. He surrendered not only all of the Americans at the fort, but also the forces under Cass and McArthur, which were in the field and could have easily escaped.

And in an act which would later be considered treason, General Hull surrendered Captain Brush's men and supplies.

His men were livid at the General's cowardice. British envoys were dispatched to the soldiers in the field to announce the surrender. Cass and McArthur were furious, but complied. Their soldiers marched as prisoners back to Detroit.

Henry Brush was an officer of a different metal.

Alexander Elliott brought him notice of the surrender. He had only two Indians to accompany him because he did not expect resistance.

Elliott expected that Brush and his men would simply surrender and march peacefully to Detroit.

Brush stated he believed that Elliott was a spy and his news was false. But a part of him knew that Hull had collapsed.

Brush arrested Elliott and threatened the Indians to make them run away.

More importantly, Captain Henry Brush immediately ordered his men to move. They were prepared and waiting.

The Indians surrounding Brush's men had been told to stand down because of the surrender.

Because no one was expecting him to do so, Brush had a chance to slip away.

A retreat has been carefully planned. Every animal was packed. Every man had been briefed. They marched south within 15 minutes of Elliott's arrival and the news of surrender.

By taking the alternate route provided by the River Rouge men, Brush was able to get a head start on any pursuers.

When Tecumseh learned that that the supply train had bolted, he sent a force to stop them. If he caught them, it would be a massacre.

Most warriors counted on taking scalps and spoils as their reward for fighting. Now that General Hull had surrendered, there was no one for them to kill.

When Tecumseh gave word they could attack and destroy Captain Brush's Company, hundreds rushed greedily after the men from Chillicothe.

The Indians assumed Brush would rush back down the new military road as quickly possible. The war party dashed down that road, but found no sign of the supply train.

Eventually they discovered the true escape path. But by then Brush had a long lead.

Corporal Joseph Cissna, Jr. took a group of 10 men on ahead of the force. One was his brother Stephen P., two were his cousins James and Joseph Cissna from Chillicothe. They rushed ahead.

Swimming the river, the Cissna cousins located the abandoned logs. It did not take long to tie them together again.

By the time Brush reached the Maumee, two rafts had been constructed and were tethered to tow ropes. Six tons of supplies were swiftly transferred and towed across. The animals were swum across in small groups until the entire company rested on the southern bank.

Once out of the Black Swamp, Brush returned to the military road and rushed back to Urbana.

They were greeted by very strange news.

First, they were heralded as heroes and praised for their escape.

Then they were informed that because of the Rules of War (of which America was strictly committed to), they were considered British prisoners.

"But I am standing right here! How can I be a prisoner?" demanded Brush. But the order stood.

They must consider themselves paroled and were not able to serve any further in the conflict. They would remain in that status until they were traded (on paper) for a British counterpart who has been taken prisoner.

At this point in the war there were no prisoners to exchange them for.

Surprisingly, more than 2,000 of the Americans surrendered at Detroit were soon to return to Urbana under the same terms.

The British commander discovered, like General Hull, that he did not have enough food to feed them all. So, while the regular soldiers were kept as prisoners, paroles were issued to the militia. They returned home the last week of August.

Brush's company was dismissed. In small groups, they returned to their homes and families in Chillicothe. Most would honor their parole and not serve again.

It must be noted that at least three men of this heroic company would serve again during the war: Captain Henry Brush himself, Lt. John Entrekin, and Stephen P. Cissna.

Under the risk of being immediately executed should they be recaptured; these men continued to fight.

Brush's men continued to be on active duty until their enlistments ran out on October 4th. They met each week at the log government building in Chillicothe to discuss their situation, and remind each other that they were prisoners-of-war.

It was a compelling cause for laughter and drinking.

CHAPTER SEVEN
Baton Rouge, Louisiana
September 1812

"thousands at his bidding speed, And post o'er land and ocean without rest; They also serve who only stand and wait."
-John Milton

In 1699, French explorer Sieur d'Iberville was leading a party up the Mississippi River. At a sharp bend in the river the dense swamps gave way to a high meadow of tall grass. At its north end, they saw a cypress pole festooned with bloody animals.

The pole was painted bright red.

They called that pole, and the place it stood guard over, Baton Rouge, or "Red Stick."

The totem was a warning of death for any that crossed the boundary between the lands of the Houma people and those of the Creek Nation north of it.

The high mound on which the "Red Stick" was placed sat at a unique place on the river. Renowned for its twists and turns, at this point the river allowed one to see several miles both up stream and down.

It was an ideal place for a military stronghold. The River Road, actually the remnant of an old buffalo trail that was hundreds of years old, came within sight of the river at this point too.

When the United States declared war on Great Britain in June of 1812, Baton Rouge still marked the boundary between nations: red nations and white nations. The land west of it had been purchased from France in the Louisiana Purchase.

But the Creek and Choctaw peoples still considered all of the land along the southern Mississippi as theirs.

Natchez, Baton Rouge, and New Orleans were the river towns that marked the edge of the Southwestern Frontier. For a nation at war, it was a very vulnerable place.

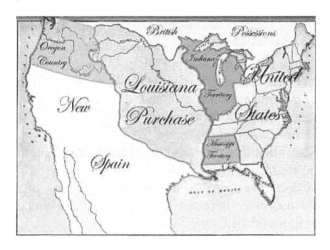

Following the Revolution, Spanish authorities had been able to shut down all American traffic on the Mississippi by simply controlling the river ports of St. Louis, New Madrid, Natchez, and Baton Rouge.

By controlling these remote locations, one could control all traffic between Pittsburgh and New Orleans. And the location made it easy to control the river with just a small force.

The Spanish fortifications at Baton Rouge were so small that a year earlier a group of immigrants from America had seized the fort. They immediately claimed all of the Spanish territory along the Gulf Coast from Mobile to Baton Rouge, and established the West Florida Republic.

It took just 90 days before the U.S. Congress objected and overpowered the new Republic in a swift annexation.

Within months, Louisiana was made a state.

When the second war with England erupted, President Madison, realized the importance of the river and its ports. He appointed Colonel Ferdinand Claiborne to raise the 3rd Infantry Regiment and secure the southwest corner of the nation.

No one knew if the area would be attacked first by the Indians inspired by Tecumseh, or by the British coming through New Orleans.

The one thing that was certain, was that the Mississippi River must remain open to American traffic. Every politician in Washington and every military minded man in the south-western region, was certain of that goal.

Word quickly spread throughout the Mississippi Territory that Claiborne was enlisting a new army. The 3rd Infantry would not be militia. They would be a part of the new U.S. Volunteers, attached directly to the Federal government and not to the state.

Law provided that the militia could only be enlisted for up to 90 days, and they were not allowed fight outside the United States. The U.S. Volunteers could be recruited for the duration of the war, and fight anywhere.

Nine companies of men would make up the regiment. Each came from a different community in the Mississippi Territory.

Young men came from homesteads throughout the forests and swamps, clamoring for the excitement of War.

The map of Mississippi Territory was deceiving. It showed the entire territory as having been ceded to the U.S. by Great Britain at the treaty of Paris. But having won access to the land from England, the Americans still had to then buy it from the Indians who lived there.

Usually this meant buying small sections purchased from one tribe after another. In Mississippi, the settlements of Americans were small and surrounded by large tracks of reserves in which the Choctaw and Creek reigned supreme.

In the map below, note that section #115 was not purchased from the Choctaw until 18 Oct 1820; #156 on 27 Sept 1830; and #178 on 20 Oct 1832.

Until those dates, the natives considered the American, French, and Spanish settlements to be reserves for the white foreigners to live on, within Indian land.

The tiny town of Port Gibson rested at the point where the Natchez Trace met the River Road (paralleling the Mississippi). From here it was a straight run down to the river port town of Natchez.

Traffic was heavy in all three directions. The people of Port Gibson were continually reminded that they were surround by a wilderness filled with savages.

The interaction between Europeans and Natives was starkly different in the south than in the north.

In the northern states, trade with the natives was highly sought after for the rich fur business. When the Spanish settled the southern areas, they saw little value in trading with the natives.

Spanish/Native relationships consisted of converting the savages to Christianity, enslaving them to work plantations, and stealing whatever gold and silver they possessed.

A visitor to Mississippi in 1810 noted that the Choctaw were a "particularly desolate people, nowhere near as noble as the black slave."

Such bigotry prevented interaction between the races from being more than tense and suspicious.

Port Gibson was filled with young men raised with terror of the vast Choctaw and Creek Nations surrounding them. Rumors that Tecumseh's war in the north was spreading to their forests had the white population on the edge of panic.

Captain John H. Shanks stepped to the center of Port Gibson and made a dramatic appeal.

The Mississippi must be made secure! An Army was needed which could interdict any Indian War which might come! Every strong young man was needed!

He raised a company of 80 men to become one of 3rd Infantry's nine companies. Enthusiasm and tempers were hot.

These young men were more than restless for a fight of any kind.

Lt. William Cessna, veteran of the Winter Campaign at Valley Forge, watched in trepidation as two of his sons stepped forward to enlist. William S. was just 21 and Culbertson D. Cessna was 18 years of age.

The boys had moved to Mississippi Territory with their father following the death of their mother, ten years prior. The Cessna home in Port Gibson was more than a little lacking in the gentilities furnished by the female touch.

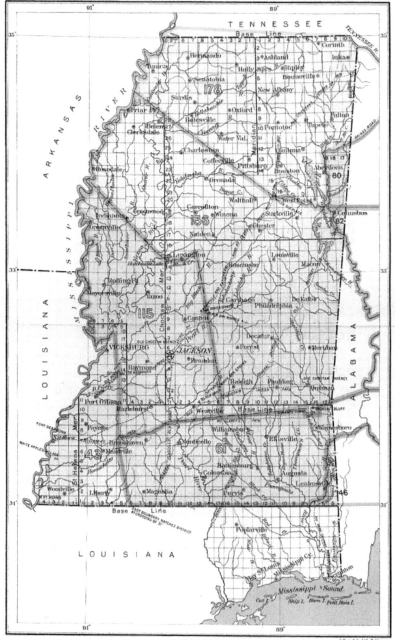

MISSISSIPPI
SCALE 35 MILES TO 1 INCH

A. Hoen & Co. Lith. Baltimore.

Joining the army seemed like a perfect life for the rough and tumble childhood they had known. Both enlisted in the U.S. Volunteer 3rd Infantry for a six-month term.

Twenty miles northeast, in the community of Utica, their 17-year-old cousin, John Cessna Neel, was enlisting in the company commanded by Captain Zachariah Lea.

Another group of young Cessna men were marching to war.

The officers of the company of 80 men raised at Port Gibson were: John H. Shanks, Capt.; William W. Blanton, 1st Lt; Peter C. Chambliss, 2nd Lt; and William Jack, ensign. Thomas Heath and John Morrison served as the company musicians, but Morrison would soon be promoted to regimental musician.

Non-commissioned officers from Port Gibson were Joseph Braden, Sgt.; James F. Scott, Sgt.; Samuel Guest, Sgt.; James H. Gowen, Sgt.; William A. Chambliss, Sgt. (Nov 30, 1812, Chambliss was promoted to Quarter Master Sgt. for the regiment); William Vance, Corp,; John Elliott, Corp.; Kinchen Carter, Corp.; and Peter McGohan, Corp.

Privates in the company included: Alexander Baldridge, James C. Beaty, Benjamin Blanton, John Bolls, John Brent, Burwell Butler, Christopher Cable, Culbertson D. Cessna, William S. Cessna, George Chapman, William Colvin, William Cook, David Davis, John Delany, Thomas Dennis, Kinsman Devine, John H. Dobbs, Peter Fait, Thomas Fake, Washington Fox, George W. Givens, John Goodrum, Thomas Goodrum, Robert Griffin, James Groves, Peter Hamberlin, Joseph Harrigill, Levi C Harris, Henry Helms, Peter Higgins, Alexander J. Hill, Alexander G. Holland, Joseph Hoinsley, Alexander Huffman, James Jones, Charles H.

Jordan, Simon Kenton*, William Kenton*, Ashly Lambert, Jacob Levertson, Thomas Marrs, John Montgomery, Christopher Murray, George W. Pentecost, John L. Platner, John Potter, John Reed, William Robinson, Nimrod Ross, William D. Sanders, Eli Scurrey, Belloup Seward, James Shannon, Thompson Shaw, Moses Shelby, Kinchen H. Shuffield, John Shull, Brice Taylor, John Terry, Thomas C. Vaughn, Oliver Wallace, John Warsaw, John Weatherly, Jacob White, Benjamin Wilson, Joseph Woods, and Allen Yokum.

Editor's Note: This may be the only complete account of the company that exists. It was gleaned from roll calls of the entire regiment.

The Kenton brothers were sons of famed frontiersman, Simon Kenton. They had wandered to Port Gibson in hopes of making money speculating in newly opened lands. Like their father, they did not like to sit in one place very long, and they loved the prospect of a fight. The Kenton and Cessna families had been friends in Pennsylvania and Kentucky since before the Revolution.

The companies met for rendezvous at Natchez and were marched 140 miles down the River Road to Baton Rouge. Their assignment was to rebuild the feeble defensives into a major supply depot and staging area for military operations in the Southwest United States. Big things were happening in Baton Rouge!

On January 1st, the *New Orleans* arrived. She became the first steamboat to navigate from Pittsburgh to New Orleans, arriving at her namesake city on January 12, 1812. She was quickly followed by dozens of steam ships of every description.

On April 30, 1812, Congress made Louisiana the 18th state and named Baton Rouge as its capital. Its culture was a mix of Creek, Spanish, French, and American. Many people from the Caribbean islands had made their way to this place as well.

The Cessna boys had never known that such a diverse community existed. An adventurous youth could find everything, from Island Rum to French tarts, and Spanish cantinas. It was an amazing place for the curious young mind. Temptations had never come in so many flavors.

For six months, the young men of the 3rd Infantry of U.S. Volunteers had little to do beside construct a large base, and watch the river. Each company took its turn conducting scouting missions throughout the forests and swamps. But no real fighting would be engaged until the Creek Wars of 1813.

Army pay was $6.66 per month. Food was good when it was available. And soon enough there were ample stores.

Some of the nine companies were set to work building earth and stone works to position cannon along the river. Some of them were set to work building the first of two huge powder magazines.

Thousands of rifles and tens of thousands of pounds of black powder would come floating down the river from the north. This had to be stored against future military actions.

Some of the companies were set to building a huge warehouse and barracks to prepare for the winter. Col Claiborne and his staff simply moved into the mansion of the Spanish Governor.

As more troops and regiments were organized in the Southwest they would be sent to Baton Rouge for training and equipage. From here they could easily be sent to defend central Alabama, Mobile, and New Orleans.

The 3rd Infantry U.S. Volunteers were used more as engineers than as combat unit. In a few months, they transformed a tiny fort into a mighty base of operations.

Their service to the war consisted of long days of watching the river and forest, and even longer days of hard construction labor.

The tension of always being ready to fight, anticipating it daily ... but it never presenting itself ... was exhausting.

And for some reason, when they were given time off for "rest and recreation" in Baton Rouge, they always returned more exhausted than when they went. And they always returned from their leave time broke!

On March 15, 1813, their mission was complete. The post at Baton Rouge was an impressive supply depot and training facility. A few of the men would enlist for another year of service.

But William S. Cessna, Culbertson D. Cessna, and John Cessna Neel felt they had given enough. In a group led by Capt. Shanks himself, they accepted discharge and travel pay of $61.16 for the 140 mile/10-day trek home.

A year later, John Shanks and John C. Neel would volunteer as privates in a company of Hinds' Dragoons raised at Utica. They would fight to take Pensacola and at the Battle of New Orleans.

But William S. and Culbertson Cessna did not accept any further military service during the war.

When William S. Cessna married Elizabeth Young on 21 Aug 1823, his former captain, John H. Shanks J.P., performed the wedding.

William and Elizabeth would bring life to the following children:

Charles C. Cessna (4 Oct 1824, lived only 10 years), Martha M. Cessna (29 Jan 1826), Elizabeth Y. Cessna (stillborn on 9 Sept 1827), William W. Cessna (12 Mar 1829), Robert A. Cessna (5 Dec 1830), Sidney S. Cessna (29 Aug 1832 but lived only 6 yrs.), Sarah "Matilda" Cessna (26 June 1834), Samantha A. Cessna (22 Oct 1836), and John L. Cessna who was born 22 Mar 1841.

Following the war, William took up land in Red Lick, Mississippi just south of Port Gibson. Sometime in the mid-1830's he relocated his family to Utica, Mississippi to live near his brother Charles.

William died a few miles north of Utica on 5 Dec 1843, having filed for his pension as a veteran of the war a few years earlier.

Culbertson D. Cessna married Margaret "Peggy" Robinette, in Red Lick, Mississippi on 28 Feb 1822. Together they would expand the Cessna clan by bearing the following children: Elizabeth Ann Cessna (1823), John Culbertson Cessna (1825), Penelope Cessna (1827), Sarah "Matilda" Cessna (1829), Charles Cessna (1831), Mary Catherine Cessna (1833), Eliza Cessna (1835), Francis "Frank" Marion Cessna (1837), Sallie Cessna and Margarite Cessna.

CHAPTER EIGHT
"Finley's Folly"
Chillicothe, Ohio
September 11, 1812

DRAFTED:

Secretary of War, William Eustis, has recommended to Congress that all men between the ages of 18 and 45 be drafted into a National Militia to be called for service in the current War with Great Britain. Governor Return J. Meigs has issued a proclamation concerning an urgent expedition to be commanded by Colonel Samuel Finley. A Regiment of Mounted Militia is being organized at Chillicothe to join the army under General William Harrison. Term of enlistment is 30 days. All men must present themselves by Sunday evening September 13, providing their own horse and equipment.

All those volunteering for this Expedition will be considered exempt from further military service during the current war.

They will also be eligible for a Bounty Land Warrant of 160 acres.

"Something smells funny about this whole thing" muttered Stephen Cissna, Sr. to himself as he read the flyer.

"This ain't the way it's done!" Stephen Cissna prided himself on being someone who knew who things "should" be done. He was a veteran of the Revolution, having served at the Battle for Boston.

He was also a man of some minor political influence, having been a part of the Chillicothe Junto and an "activist" group called "Baldwin's Bloodhounds." The latter had been very active (even violent) during the political tumult which brought statehood to Ohio.

Stephen Cessna, Sr. had the distinction of being one of the few men in this city who had sent four sons to fight in this war that was barely three months old. He felt he was a bit more knowledgeable than most.

As he pondered the proclamation further, other things struck him as strange.

The enlistment was for only 30 days, not the duration of the mission. The promised reward was for 160 acres of land; but this had previously only been promised to those who enlisted for 5 years in the regular Army.

And the Commander, Samuel Finley, was not an officer in the usual sense. Samuel Finley was the 60-year-old President of the Bank of Chillicothe.

It was true that Finley was a close friend and political ally of Governor Meigs. And it was not unheard of for old men who had political ambitions to be given gratuitous rank during times of war.

But the only command that Finley had ever held was as the Quartermaster for the May 14, 1778, muster, of the Sixth Battalion of Cumberland County Pennsylvania Militia.

There were a number of veterans from the Bedford and Cumberland County militias in Chillicothe. They had never considered Sam Finley to be a real soldier.

Something smelled false and suspicious about the entire affair.

But that did not stop another of Stephen Cissna, Sr.'s sons from enlisting. William Cissna, his 31-year-old son with Elizabeth Barnhill, showed up Sunday evening with a borrowed horse and pistol.

He was hastily placed in a company commanded by Captain Jacob Bell. Because he did not come with a rifle or musket he was designated the company musician.

No one could explain to him why a company of mounted militia would need a musician, or even what instrument he was supposed to play. William thought the title sounded prestigious so he was happy.

Stephen Cissna, Sr. instantly became an important personage in the town of Chillicothe. He had now provided five sons to serve in this war.

Six sons, if you counted John who served as a teamster. This was more than any other man in the city. And the war was not even three months old.

The expedition did not bother to provide any training. No inspection was done of their equipment and weapons.

No one even counted to see how many rounds of ammunition each man had bought with him. At first light on Monday morning, Colonel Samuel Finley rode out at the head of a column of eager volunteers.

The Chillicothe Gazette reported the event like this: *On Monday last, General Samuel Finley, left this place, for the purpose of joining General Harrison in his contemplated expedition, accompanied by about 150 mounted riflemen musketeers.*

On October 3rd, the Gazette carried this story: *General Samuel Finley has resigned the presidency of the Bank in Chillicothe in consequence of his engaging in an expedition against the enemies of his country. General Thomas Worthington has been elected to supply the vacancy thus occasioned.*

Stephen Cissna, Sr., who paid close attention to military details, did not miss that the newspaper had promoted Sam Finley from Colonel to General.

The Expedition made all haste to catch up with General William Harrison deep in the woods of Northern Indiana.

His army was involved in a slow and exhausting march up the Wabash River to Fort Wayne and from there on to the Falls of the Maumee. Once there he would launch an attack on Detroit and Canada.

But the going had been very tough. Following the example of General Anthony Wayne of twenty years earlier; he was cautious.

Harrison was building a series of forts along the river trail. He left each of them filled with as many supplies as he could. So, the amount of food and ammunition he had, got smaller with every depot he left behind him. The size of his army got small with every detachment of men he left at each fort.

Progress was further slowed by the constant harassment of the Indian Army under Tecumseh.

Every day Harrison was sending some small force out to burn a village or to respond to some threat. Tecumseh was doing his best to bog the army down, and delay any invasion of Canada.

"Harass and Delay" was the strategy of Great War Chief.

And as summer faded, so did what little fresh pasture his animals could find in the dense woodlands. His pack animals were failing badly.

Every day the army and its pack train had to chop their way through swamps, ravines, and briars. By early December so many of the animals were broken, and had to be put-down, that Harrison reported a loss of half a million dollars in livestock.

Supplies were being carried on sleds pulled by the men themselves.

Private William Cissna, "Company Musician," had little idea what he was really doing. Every morning he got up when Captain Bell told them to. He rode behind the officers all day long. He unfolded his bedroll wherever they told him to at night.

When they finally caught up with Harrison's army the last week of September it was not anything that he expected.

William had hoped to find his brother, Charles who was a sergeant with the 19th Infantry. But the Army was scattered over about 50 square miles of forest.

Captain Bell was told to camp his men along the Auglaize River and wait for orders. Colonel Samuel Finley, just disappeared.

Obviously, he was meeting with General Harrison, but no one was really sure where headquarters was.

And no one could tell William Cissna where his brother's company might be located in the vast and dense woods.

On October 14th, Colonel Finley returned to his men. He promptly issued them official discharges. Their term of service was as promised, 30 days.

He then issued them orders they had not expected.

They were being discharged (abandoned) at the River Auglaize, 200 miles from their home. They were on their own to get back.

And to add insult, their horses were going to be kept by the Army. They would have to walk home. And it was one of the worst winters that Ohio had ever known.

Walking home would be a cold and hungry experience. What had once been an army of mounted men, was now a scattering of small groups of men, walking home.

Colonel Finley and his staff kept their mounts and would make a swift return to Chillicothe. But Captain Bell and the men would have to walk their way home.

The obvious truth was that Harrison's army did not need more mouths to feed. He especially did not need militia men who had no training and poor weapons.

Harrison did, however, need more horses to carry the supplies he did have. After three months of carrying loads through untracked forests, most of his pack animals had worn out.

The Chillicothe Gazette carried this story on October 24: *General Samuel Finley has been elected president of the Bank in Chillicothe in the place of General Thomas Worthington has resigned.*

What seemed obvious (but was not the truth) was that Samuel Finley had used personal influence to gain himself a little "Glory." Rumor was that he had hoped to talk his old friend William Harrison into giving him a command position.

But General Harrison had simply said, "No, thank you" and sent him back home.

The truth was an entirely different matter.

Things were not going as General Harrison had expected. He was using up his stores much faster than Governor Meigs and the War Department could resupply. Winter was coming and it was becoming obvious to the strategists that the plan to invade Canada that Fall was in jeopardy.

In July, General Hull had allowed his personal papers to be captured by the enemy. All of the United States' detailed plans to invade Canada were revealed.

Governor Return J. Meigs and Secretary of War, William Eustis had no intention of allowing that to happen again.

"Finley's Folly" as it became known in the taverns of the Ohio Capital, was really a secret mission to evaluate and update the war plan.

In the newspapers (which might fall into enemy hands) it was presented that an arrogant old banker was chasing glory. Even the elevation of his rank to "General" was a collaboration of the paper to add to the ruse.

The real mission was to get an honest evaluation of what General Harrison hoped to accomplish before winter set in. It was decided between Harrison and Finley that week; that invasion of Canada was not a possibility for 1812.

Publicly, Harrison gave every intention of retaking Detroit before Christmas. But strategically, he had decided that the rest of that year would need to be spent gathering men and supplies.

"I need one million rations of food before I can consider invading Canada." Harrison wrote to Governor Meigs and William Eustis. That message was carried in person by Colonel Samuel Finley.

Because the secret explanation was never revealed, the expedition known as "Finley's Folly" ruined Samuel Finley's political career. Several times he ran for office. But he was never again entrusted with public leadership.

When the Panic of 1819 set in, Finley's land investments became mired and he was frequently sued by the United States Bank to have his property sold at Marshall's sales. He eventually quit the community of Chillicothe in embarrassment and went to live with his daughter in Philadelphia.

His obituary in the Chillicothe Gazette on 16 April 1829 stated that he had "a long and checkered life."

William Cissna married Margrate Hall on 19 March 1815 in the community of London in Madison County, by Burton Blizzard, JP.

Private William Cissna was among the first to apply for bounty land as soon as the war was over. On December 31, 1817, he was granted a patent for land in Bureau County, Illinois. He sold it immediately to a land speculator named Colonel Joseph Watson. The sale was made in Chillicothe and Cissna never saw the land he sold.

His life following the war is mysterious. Speculation about his life is included as a chapter titled "Dr. William Cissna" of the next book in the Our America Series, *Where Will We Prosper.*

Editor's Note: Secretary of War, William Eustis had recommended to Congress that a military draft be instituted. Congress disagreed and no draft was ever called. Privates William Cissna, William Coddington, and William Curry each wrote their Bounty Land Application that they had been drafted but opted for the Finley Expedition when they were promised they would not have to provide further service in the war.

CHAPTER NINE
Chillicothe, OH
14 September 1812

The flatboat was tied up along the banks of the Scioto River. Just a few yards stood the two-story log building known as "The Barracks." Four, armed militia men stood in constant guard. They rotated in three hour shifts.

They were men from Captain Henry Brush's company. No one seemed to mind that they were technically British Prisoners-of-War. They were there to guard against theft. It was very unlikely that British soldiers would come marching into the Capitol of Ohio.

On the boat one could make out sixty long wooden boxes. They were simply marked "Harper's Ferry, VA." Inside each box lay ten brand new muskets, complete with bayonets, cartridge boxes, and leather shoulder straps.

They were supposed to be a secret cargo, but everyone in town knew what they were.

The United States had not kept a large standing army following the Revolution. Yet she had not let the possibility of war fade from her mind.

The mindset of every American was that a hastily-called militia of free men would always be able to overpower an army of paid soldiers. But they would need weapons. America was a country preoccupied with a need for weapons.

Most militia simply showed up equipped with their old hunting rifles and shotguns. Congress intended to equip them with more appropriate weapons whenever possible.

The U.S. Armories at Harper's Ferry, Virginia and Springfield, Massachusetts had been steadily producing 10,000 muskets every year. These were stored against a future need.

And they were needed now.

Model 1806 Musket from Harper's Ferry Armory

But they were not needed on a boat in Chillicothe. They were needed in Indiana. The 19th Infantry Regiment had completed training at Zanesville and were now under forced march to relieve the fort at Vincennes, in Indiana Territory.

This was a precious cargo which needed to be moved, and moved quickly.

If the relief column left immediately, they could intercept the 19th Infantry on their way to Indiana. New weapons would make an important addition to the potency of this regiment.

Urbana was 80 miles away, through thick forests. The old buffalo trail was hardly much of a road at all. And for several months now, Shawnee and Miami war parties had been seen scouting this part of the country.

Governor Meigs had only one source of manpower that might handle the job of escorting the shipment safely to the army in Indiana. However, there was a problem.

The only organized, armed, and experienced group of men available to him were the men of Henry Brush's company. They were still under enlistment until

October. But technically, they were prisoners of war who had been paroled.

By rules of war they could not serve again until the war ended or they were traded on paper for British soldiers.

If they were captured again, and if the enemy recognized them as parolees, they could be executed on the spot.

It was a serious danger for these men to be asked for further duty. They could not, and would not be taken alive!

But Governor Meigs asked them even so. And twenty men of the company stepped forward to volunteer. It would only take a couple of weeks, but that did not alter their risk.

Craighead Ferguson was promoted to Lieutenant and designated as the group's commander. Stephen P. Cissna also stepped forward to volunteer. Together they returned to active duty on September 14 of 1812. They would return to Chillicothe on September 28th and once again assume their status of prisoner-of-war.

The adventure was uneventful except for two things. Stephen P.'s cousin, John Cissna would hire on to serve as teamster. This would be his first participation in the war.

John was the son of Stephen Cissna who had fought with Washington at the Battle for Boston.

John was anxious to visit the 19th Regiment. He wanted to visit his brother who served in the Army unit there. John also took along his 12-year-old son Robert to help him in his teamster responsibilities.

John Cissna had no reason to think this was a combat mission. The trip was uneventful and hurried. Delivery was made as planned, and the group returned to Chillicothe in just over two weeks.

Young Robert Cissna would remember this trip as his great adventure at war. He would often recount that his father was "Captain of the Teamsters" during this adventure.

John carried letters to Charles Cissna from his wife Dorcus. A reconciliation of sort was completed as his wife informed and consulted Charles about their business affairs through these letters.

They made terrific partners, even if they could not live under the same roof while their spirits were hot and young.

Dorcus thrived as head of the household in Charles' absence.

On his return, John Cessna carried letters of reconciliation to his sister-in-law.

CHAPTER TEN
Fort Meigs, Ohio
January 1, 1813

This had been the hardest year of Sergeant Charles Cissna's life. He had seen bad winters, but never experienced anything like he was enduring now.

Winter had come early this year. As General Harrison's army fought its way up the Wabash, to Fort Wayne, and then down the Maumee River, winter caught up with them.

The going had already been difficult enough before the cold set in. There were no roads on their march. Cannons and supply wagons had to be dragged and manhandled through forests and swamps. Often, they had to be disassembled to be carried across streams and rivers.

As fall gave way to a deep blanket of snow, there was no fodder for the animals save what the army carried. The horses began to suffer greatly. By December 10th most of the horses were broken down so badly they had to be destroyed.

The army reported loss of half a million dollars by the animals "put down" that week.

The men were not in much better shape. Winter clothing had not caught up with them yet. Supply lines were a mess and most of the men were without any protection against the cold except for wrapping blankets around themselves.

The men of the Kentucky militia were still wearing their linen hunting shirts. The 19th Infantry Regiment had worn out their first pair of shoes in just four months and some of them were barefoot.

The Army cooks were foraging in the woods to supplement the meals with nuts, because they had run out of flour long before. Most of the meat they carried was spoiled, but they served it anyway.

By Christmas, all the rivers in northern Indiana, Ohio, and Michigan were frozen solid. The army built sleds to drag their supplies through the forest.

But with the horses in such bad shape, most of these had a team of five men dragging them slowly along.

General William Henry Harrison had one clear goal: to retake Detroit, Mackinac, Fort Dearborn (Chicago), and to take Canada from the British. He intended to do it only once. So, his planning was very meticulous.

The entire autumn of 1812 had been one with the status of "danger close." As the army moved up the Wabash and down the Maumee, the natives continued to harass its weaker points every day.

The 19th and 17th Infantries burned and destroyed every Indian village they could find. Usually, the natives would simply retreat from their towns, returning in small raiding parties to punish whatever isolated soldiers they could find.

It was demanding work every day, with no rest, and with no chance to let down one's guard -- because death could be hiding around the next tree.

And worst of all, the army was sick.

Most of the companies were decimated by sick call. Carrying the sick was just another burden on already overburdened soldiers. It was a constant struggle to keep the healthy, healthy.

Nightly, they had to clear away a foot of snow to find some cold wet ground to sleep on. They got so wet that it hardly seemed worth the effort to pitch their tents; most just collapsed near the fire each night.

But some nights it was even impossible to find enough dry wood to make a fire.

By January 1st Harrison accepted the fact which his entire army knew. There was no way to make an assault on Detroit that winter. The army was just too worn out, and had too few supplies.

He decided to make for tiny Fort Meigs a base of operations for his assault on the British forces. It stood on the south side of the Maumee River at modern day Perrysburg, Ohio.

He wrote to his commanders that he needed at least one million rations of food, stored at Ft. Meigs, before he could begin an invasion of Canada.

Immediately his exhausted troops set to work building defenses and shelters for the coming winter. The military road built by General Hull eight months earlier was now flooded with supply wagons.

Crossing the Black Swamp, which spread to the southeast of the fort, in winter presented a roadblock which slowed down the flow.

Fort Meigs would become the largest military armory and supply depot in Ohio.

As the men worked feverously to complete the task, the woods around them teamed with native war parties. The Indians hoped to find some American alone or in a small party. It was a very tense time.

The army had advanced toward Fort Meigs in two columns. General Harrison's force marched up the right side.

About 10 miles distant, Colonel Winchester's force, mostly made up of the 17th Infantry and Kentucky militia, struggled up the left. They were the most exhausted and starving part of the army. And they were the closest to collapsing in exhaustion.

As Harrison was settling in at Fort Meigs, Col. Winchester was desperately worried about his men. He heard that a short way from him, at Frenchtown, there was a supply of flour and meat.

But he was also told that the British had been coming there to steal the supplies and that soon it would all be gone.

Splitting his force, Winchester pushed to Frenchtown on the River Raisin. It was within 25 miles of Detroit. After a brief skirmish on January 18th, his men seized the town and its supplies. They fell on the food they found and devoured nearly all of it.

The resistance they had met from the Canadian Militia had been stubborn but light. Somehow the Americans felt secure in their position.

However, the officers knew their defenses were far from adequate. Much of their perimeter was made up of picket or rail fences. And they were down to about 20 rounds of ammunition per man.

General Harrison could see their vulnerability with half their force in the woods and half only partially dug in Frenchtown. The half holding the town was split again with men camped on both sides of the frozen Raisin.

General Harrison had not approved of Winchester's assault on the town, but was pleased with the success. He ordered three more companies of the 17th and one company of the 19th to reinforce Winchester at Frenchtown.

Sergeant Charles Cissna was third in command of the company from the 19th.

Col Winchester ordered the regular army troops to camp outside the perimeter of the town, making up the first line of defense. Half of them were on each side of the frozen river.

In the predawn of January 22, a large force of 597 British regulars and Canadian militia, and 800 of Tecumseh's warriors, walked across the frozen Detroit River and attacked the Americans at Frenchtown. Fighting was fierce and bloody.

When it became obvious that success was improbable, the American officers chose to surrender. Many of the men from Kentucky objected violently, stating that they would rather die fighting than be massacred by the Indians as prisoners.

With assurances from the British officer that they would be safe, the American officers surrendered their men.

Over the next two days, though, a terrible massacre ensued. As they were being marched back to Fort Malden, Tecumseh's men would fall upon the helpless Americans and slaughter them.

Tecumseh himself did intervene to stop the killing, but not before more than 300 of the prisoners had been butchered. The second battle of the Frenchtown would become known as "The Massacre of the River Raisin."

"Remember the Raisin" would serve as a rallying cry throughout the remaining months of war.

Later, Brigadier General James Winchester reported that 547 of his men were taken as prisoners and only 33 of those escaped the battlefield to be held as prisoners of war at Fort Malden.

The company of the 19th Regulars was stationed on the southeast perimeter. Early in the battle they found themselves cut off by an eager group of savages that had charge in between them and the town. They were now fighting enemy on every side.

The Lieutenant and Ensign were both gravely wounded. Sergeant Charles Cissna found himself in command.

Although they were later called heroic, most of his actions that day were committed in desperation. There were more enemy between him and Frenchtown than there were between himself and Ft. Meigs.

The choice seemed obvious. He ordered his men to beat a hasty retreat 30 miles to the Maumee River. His choice saved his company from the massacre which followed.

The only safety Sgt. Cissna and his men would find was in speed. The woods were filled with war parties, swarming around the Americans like hornets.

When they broke up into small groups they were attacked by opportunistic groups of warriors. Charles Cissna had his hands full in keeping his men bunched together.

If his column moved quickly enough, they could get to Fort Meigs before a larger group of Indians could be sent from the main battle to chase them.

Sgt. Cissna pushed his men as hard as he could. They reached safety before sundown, having retreated 30 miles in about 10 hours. Sergeant Charles Cissna turned 30 years old a few days later.

General Harrison felt personally devastated at the defeat on River Raisin. But he used it as a public relations tool to bolster his cause on the home front.

Harrison declared the army "At Winter Quarters" and launched no more actions. He began to strengthen his force by resting and feeding the weary, and waiting for new troops to arrive. Supplies began to flow across the frozen roads and pile up in their store houses.

The 26th Regiment from Vermont made its way into Fort Meigs in late February. They had lost some officers on their march there, and Sgt. Charles Cissna was tapped for promotion.

He was promoted to Ensign, or 3rd Lieutenant, and assigned to the 26th. His experience was used to help prepare these new men for the fighting to come.

Harrison steadily built his forces in preparation for a summer assault on Detroit and Canada when spring came.

Ensign Charles Cissna spent the winter weeks getting rested and putting some flesh back on his bare bones.

As he looked at the Vermont men he was to turn into soldiers, a unique experience came over him. As would happen to millions of American soldiers in centuries to come. Six months of combat changed him.

He became a dedicated soldier. He fell into that mindset that hardened soldiers find.

He no longer wondered if he would survive this war. He resigned himself that he would die in the prosecution of it. He accepted his death as a certainty and resolved to give his best effort. It was now a question of "when" he would die, not "if."

At this point, it is only courage and dedication which make a soldier rise each morning.

CHAPTER ELEVEN
Chillicothe, Ohio
13 April 1813

It had been a long hard winter for Harrison's army at Fort Meigs. Supplies had been steadily coming in and relief troops were swelling the size of the army. But every shipment was hard fought.

While the British and Americans did not take the field in the terrible weather conditions, Tecumseh's warriors did. Every supply train or new regiment had to fight through a gauntlet of surprise ambushes to get to the massive supply depot.

The attacks were not large, but they were frequent, rapid, and deadly.

There was no way to let one's guard down.

In Chillicothe, John Cissna was hiring out for the third time as a teamster for a supply train to Fort Meigs. It did not matter to him what he was carrying, the pay was good.

For a second time, he decided to take his son, Robert, with him. The boy was now 13 and had grown to near man size.

The work being hard and the risk of losing his livestock being great, it seemed a prudent thing to have extra help.

On April 13, 1813, the Cissna father and son team left Chillicothe for another trip up Hull's military road. It was sure to be difficult getting through the Black Swamp in the wet spring.

John's father, Stephen Cissna, Sr., the veteran of the Battle of Boston, watched them leave with deep concern. Beside him on the tavern porch was Stephen Cissna, Jr., broken in body from his experience at the first blush of war. Neither of them was happy to see John and Robert depart.

The trip was hard. The difficulty came partly from the hurry they were in, and partly from the unpredictable weather.

Several times they were drenched by spring downpours. Once, they cowered under cover from a ferocious thunderstorm that northern Ohio is famous for.

In the past week, they had seen more and more Indians shadowing them in the forest. Two days from Fort Meigs, the savages made their first attack. They would make three more before the convoy was safely within the fort.

A group of about 40 Wyandot and Shawnee ambushed the last 10 men in the supply train. One was killed. Two were injured before enough firepower could be directed at them to make the warriors retreat.

Robert Cissna ran to where his father had been knocked from his horse. John Cissna was shot through one lung and having great difficulty breathing. The ball had passed straight through.

But he now had a hole in the front and back which was preventing that lung from functioning.

He was treated in a rushed manner. Buckskin patches were lashed over both wounds so he could breathe, and he was placed on a litter for the rest of the trip. Bullets still flew over their heads.

Robert walked in horror beside his father's litter the last 20 miles to Fort Meigs. He had no way of knowing if his father would live or die. And he had no real power to affect either outcome.

In those two days, Robert Cissna transformed for boyhood to manhood at age 13. Using his father's rifle, he returned fire at the fleeting savages in the woods.

At the fort, the regimental surgeon treated John, and reported that he might survive. His brother, Ensign Charles Cissna, now of the 26th Regiment from Vermont, assumed guardianship of young Robert until John recovered.

But the excitement was far from over.

On May 1, 1813, a British force of regulars, Canadian militia, and over a thousand warriors commanded by Tecumseh launched an attack on Fort Meigs. John and Robert Cissna were trapped and unable to return to Chillicothe even should John be healthy enough.

The siege lasted until May 9th and ended with the British withdrawing in frustration.

Tecumseh's warriors were not good at siege fighting. They lost interest very quickly if there was no direct fighting going on.

Satisfied that he had given the Americans a strong warning to advance no further, the British commander withdrew.

John and Robert could now go home. They arrived back in Chillicothe exactly 45 days after they left. That was the final contribution that either father or son made to the war effort.

Ensign Charles Cissna would soon start a year of constant campaigning against the British.

Two follow-up stories are important for this chapter.

The first is that John Cissna would die on 3 September 1821. Reports of his demise state that the wound he received in the war was a major cause of his death. His lung never functioned correctly again, and in a weakened state, he could not withstand the viral invasion of that fall.

The second is a story, told not by Robert but by his second wife. Government records report her long application and subsequent denial for pension benefits and bounty land rights as Robert's widow.

She ascribes his service as being under both Captain John Cissna and Captain John Entreken. None of her assertions could be substantiated by the War Department.

The children of Robert's first marriage sent an affidavit to the Pension Office.

They state that Robert was never enlisted and had only been 13 years at the time he served. Hired teamsters were civilians and not due any pension or land bounty.

That is why Robert Cissna did not appear on any army roster even though he had been under fire defending army supplies.

They further stipulate that their father left his second wife very well off and that she was not anywhere near needing pension benefits.

CHAPTER TWELVE
Bedford, Pennsylvania
23 April 1813

"Men! They need help at Erie!" shouted Andrew Sheets. He was standing on the courthouse steps in Bedford, Pennsylvania.

"They need that help now!"

"If we don't go and help 'em, the Brits will overrun the place and be down here in our back yard within a fortnight. I ain't gonna let them come and take our homes from us. We worked too hard to build this country."

Andrew Sheets then launched a short monologue of invectives demonstrating how much he disapproved of living under the rule of King and Parliament.

He concluded with the battle cry: "To Erie!"

He began to march from the courthouse to the bridge over the Juniata, and back again. Men fell into a mob behind him.

They were supposed to be falling into neat ranks which would impress their neighbors. But having been drinking in the taverns most of the day, few were able to keep rhythm or judge distance between themselves and their marching buddies.

There were numerous Revolutionary War heroes and veteran Indian fighters in this community.

Too old for war, most men had sons who were at the prime age. Bedford had been at the center of much of the fighting during the War for Independence.

Patriot fervor was a staple in every household.

There were probably 30 Cessna men of fighting age in this county. Only one would volunteer.

Curiously, none of the children or grandchild of renowned community leader, Major John Cessna, would serve in this war.

The only Pennsylvania Cessna to serve during these 36 months of conflict was William Franklin Cessna.

His grandfather was Colonel Charles Cessna of the Bedford Militia, brother of Major John. His father was Captain Charles Cessna, Jr. who had served as an aide to Col. Charles during the war.

At the age of 27, William Franklin Cessna had never left his father's home. He had not taken a wife or started his own homestead. As he listened to the words of Andrew Sheets his heart was stirred.

William had never done anything important with his life. He had never done anything dramatic and heroic like his father and grandfather.

This seemed like his calling to importance. So, he fell in line beside his childhood friends.

William F. Cessna was off to war.

The British had six well-built fighting ships above the Niagara Falls. With these they were dominating Lakes Erie, Michigan, Huron, and Superior as well as the Detroit River and Lake St. Clair.

After a year of fighting, America knew she would not be able to effectively invade Canada, without naval support. Nor could she hold on to any of the important forts along the lakes. The northern border was very vulnerable.

America needed a freshwater navy.

Daniel Dobbins was sent by Congress to complete the daunting task of building an American Navy on the upper lakes.

But there were no shipyards. There were no men experienced in building anything more than small vessels.

Dobbins chose Presque Isle, a sandy fishhook of land near Erie, Pennsylvania. It offered a calm harbor and an abundance of old-growth oak trees in nearby forests. And he gathered the best workmen he could to build a fleet of war ships.

The new shipyards were extremely vulnerable. It wouldn't be hard for the British to move two gunships into the bay and destroy all of his work.

Presque Isle needed to be fortified. All the Army's regiments were busy elsewhere. So, the militia was called out.

Captain Andrew Sheet's company joined several others to form a Regiment under the leadership of militia Colonel David Royal. They pledged to serve for just six months. Congress hoped six months would give them time to raise additional regular army troops for the job.

Each man passed a cursory physical exam. He had to demonstrate that his shoes were adequate for the march ahead. And each had to bring his own weapon.

An amazing assortment of firearms showed up with the men. Some were one of a kind and had to have the ammunition specially made for their own gun. These men carried a bullet mold matched to their musket and would have to manufacture their own ammunition.

The quartermaster furnished paper and powder for them to make their own cartridges. Most of them carried the very same tomahawks which their fathers and grandfathers had carried in the first war with England.

Off they marched.

The road from Pittsburgh to Presque Isle had seen many armies and war parties march its length. But it was still hardly more than an overgrown dirt path. It was not an easy march for men who were only used to farm labor.

When they arrived at Erie, they were told there were no barracks available to them. They were assigned to an unsecured area of the forest and told to "dig in."

Units like theirs were placed in a protective circle around the boat works, lest the British try to send a force through to destroy them. Accommodations for the troops were haphazard and constructed with whatever the men could find.

Nothing was uniform. Nothing was adequate enough to provide warm and dry shelter.

Kitchens and sanitary facilities were constructed by each company according to the whims of their officers. Few of the supervising officers really understood the importance of careful construction for these essentials to camp life.

Food and supplies were sporadic in their delivery. Usually they only came when the officers went to the regimental Quartermaster and railed about the inattention his company was receiving.

They had been in camp a few weeks when disturbing news was handed to the men. They were told that some Army regulation meant that they could no longer stay under the leadership of Captain Sheets and Colonel Royal.

The entire company was transferred to a Regular Army light artillery regiment commanded by Major Green. Captain Samuel Thomas would be their new company commander.

The men were both furious and troubled.

Militia men were accustomed to choosing the men under whom they would fight. It was one element that bound them together when times "got difficult."

They were fighting for and with friends. The men who ordered them into harm's way were men they had a long history of confidence in.

Now they would fight for strangers; and regular stiff-necked army officers at that. Morale sank deeply for William and his friends.

But the move turned out to be a good one in the end.

Regular army officers knew how to construct a camp. Sanitation improved. Quality of food improved. They were given tents and placed in a camp formation which made sense and order. And they were moved back from the edge of forest.

The artillery companies were arranged surrounding the boat works. They had the boat builders at their back and the front-line soldiers before them.

William Cessna's company was kept on the dryer high grounds and not close to the swamps.

The fall of 1813 was a bad one for the average soldier. Most of those troops stationed around the Great Lakes were close to swamps and marshes.

From those wetlands, a long sizzling summer produced a vast host of mosquitos. As a result, malaria hit the troops hard that summer. And with the coming fall a new epidemic hit the country.

"Cold Fever," a type of typhoid, swept the country. It was a bacterial infection that came from water or food that was contaminated by fecal material.

With so many armies and war parties marching through the northern forests, much of the water was contaminated. The shortage of whiskey or rum to "purify" the drinking water complicated things even more.

By October, the epidemic was so large that considerable numbers of settlers were abandoning their frontier homes. The frontline soldiers, living where sanitation was more difficult to attain, were struck heavily with the "Cold Fever."

Private William F. Cessna escaped this epidemic. He had the blessing of being in an artillery company where officers were fussy about the slightest details. Though he complained about the regimented life he was living, it prevented him from much harm and danger.

The Bedford, Pennsylvania men marveled at how quickly the boat yard was producing new craft. Every week they could visit among the construction and see the amazing transformation. Before there eyes oak skeletons were growing into impressive war ships.

In mid-August, the *USS Lawrence*, a 493-ton brig, sailed out of the boat yards. Oliver Perry, the navy commander, assumed its captaincy and named it as his flag ship.

The Americans now had a fighting force on Lake Erie. But it was only one fighting ship.

The *U.S.S. Niagara*, a near twin of the *Lawrence*, was next to sail out just a few days later. Several other ships were quick to follow. To the militia posted around the shipyards, it seemed like a new ship was launched every week.

An exact replica of the U.S.S. Lawrence.

On 10 September 1813 Perry's command met a British squadron of ships at Put-In Bay. This was a small inlet on an island in Lake Erie, just north of Sandusky, Ohio. Fighting like a bulldog. Perry was successful, but not before his flag ship was disabled.

Perry jumped into a small boat, and had his men row him half a mile through the combative waters to the *Niagara*. Cannon fire sailed all around him.

Transferring his flag to that ship, he renewed the attack and prevailed. The commander of the British ships began to realize that he was being outfought by a force much smaller than his own. He reluctantly surrendered.

It was the first time in history an entire British squadron had surrendered. All of those captured ships now became part of the American Navy.

The number of fighting ships and the amount of food and munitions quadrupled in that one afternoon. And that single afternoon changed the entire course of the war in the north.

In the previous week, the British Navy had threatened the existence of every American fort along the southern shores of the Great Lakes. This week, those same ships were flying American flags and posed a severe threat to every Canadian and British fort along the northern shores.

On 15 September, Private William Franklin Cessna and a vast crowd of militia men watched in awe as Perry returned his new fleet to Presque Isle. They were escorting six captured British vessels: two ships, two brigs, one schooner, and one sloop.

The population of Erie, Pennsylvania erupted in celebration. Every civilian and military person in the area was ecstatic!

Soon the entire nation was celebrating. The British no longer controlled the upper lakes. Now they would have to abandon their forts at Detroit and Amerherstburg.

Military strategies changed.

And they dramatically changed the life of Private William Franklin Cessna. A smaller number of troops would be sufficient to guard Presque Isle. Most of the troops were made available for other theatres of conflict.

Major Green's artillery was ordered to Sandusky to help strengthen Fort Stephenson.

Being soldiers, they were told to march there, rather than be transported by ship. So, they made the long arduous journey through the forests along northern Ohio.

They crossed swamps and rivers using pure determination and hard labor.

That is where William Franklin met the enemy which that would eventually take his life.

It was a mosquito. The last week of September, it infected him with malaria.

About the 1st of October, just as the artillery regiment was camping along the River Carrion, William fell ill.

It began with a headache.

George Caster, William's messmate noticed that he was not functioning like he should. Soon a fever overtook him and he simply collapsed. As Caster and others moved him to a pallet in a tent, he began to shiver and convulse uncontrollably.

The regimental surgeon was called and quickly pronounced that he was being attacked by "ague" (malaria). He was moved to the hospital where he lay with about two dozen other men who had contracted the same ailment.

His illness would come and go for the rest of his life. Every time it recurred, it left him weaker.

The attack usually lasted two to three days. During the high fever days William was absolutely helpless. He would alternate between high fever and fits of vomiting.

Other parts of his body began to lose fluids as well, as the immune system tried to flush out the invader. On those days, he dared not wear pants and wandered around with just a blanket for modesty. He was a horrible specter of a man.

This was followed by a period when he was shivering with chills that brought convulsions. He would be fast in bed for several days.

The attack would eventually pass and William would be extremely weak for a week. Then he could resume his duties for a time. But he constantly complained about pain in his joints and lower back.

Like most of the soldiers "attacked by ague" he would rotate in and out of the hospital, performing his duty when he was able.

On November 1st, the commander at Lower Sandusky declared that their six-month enlistment was complete. Every one of the boys from Bedford was given a carefully prepared certificate of discharge and released from duty.

As a group, they started a light-hearted journey home. It would be a 400-mile walk. But waiting for them was home and hearth.

A week into their journey, William Cessna was struck down again with fever. And he was not alone. Lack of sleep and exposure to the elements set them up for a recurrence.

About ten of the Bedford boys had the same illness. They would succumb to fever and chills at various points along the road home.

The group was anxious to get home. Carrying William seemed like an unnecessary burden. Besides, he would get well quicker if he had a warm place to rest.

George Caster located a farmer in the area who promised to nurse Cessna back to health for a small fee. The course of his illness was pretty predictable. He would either die or recover in just a few days.

Cessna was left at an isolated farm in the woods of northern Ohio while his friends marched home.

William Franklin Cessna, or what remained of him, staggered into Bedford, Pennsylvania exactly four weeks after his company.

Private Cessna had been "attacked by Ague" twice on his return and had to find a place to rest and recover. Once home, he retired to his parent's home and was confined by illness until spring.

He never was the same strong young man again.

The malaria had settled into his joints. A part of his lower spine was continually inflamed.

He might go for weeks or months functioning well. But if he got wet or cold, or simply exposed to the elements too long, he was soon sick again.

Pvt. Cessna and the rest of the company had still not received any of the pay which had been promised to them.

In the summer of 1814, the Bedford boys were told that if they wished to collect back pay owed to them they would need to go to the Nation's Capitol at Pittsburgh. When they presented documentation of discharge, the paymaster would give them what was owed.

William Cessna was completely unable to travel. He delivered his discharge certificate to a friend, Martin Riley. Riley promised to collect his pay and return with the same.

Cessna never saw or heard from Riley again. He might have suspected dishonesty, but the truth was that many lone travelers in the western area just disappeared during those years. Danger still lurked in the forests.

In 1851, William Franklin Cessna applied for pension based on the illness he had contracted in the war. It had never left him in peace for more than a few months at a time. George Caster entered a deposition at this time, confirming the details of his military experience.

Doctors Samuel Kelly and Wm. Barnett conducted an examination and confirmed the details of his affliction and the nature of his disability.

William was never able to be self-sufficient. He lived with his parents until their deaths. Then he was taken in by his sister, Rachael McCauslin, who cared for him until his death in 1862.

After surviving dozens of bouts with "Ague," his 76-year-old body had just run short of strength to fight the fever. He had never married or been able to provide for a family.

Though not listed among the war dead, William Franklin Cessna was among its casualties.

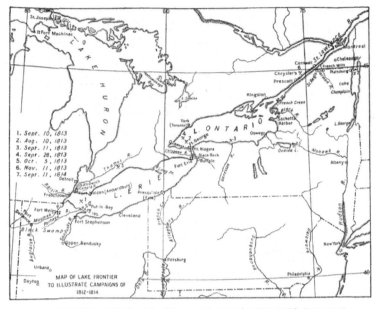

From "Seapower in Its Relation to the War of 1812 (Vol. 1, p. 371) by A.T. Mahan (Boston: Little, Brown, 1905).

CHAPTER THIRTEEN
Fort Meigs, Ohio
May 1813

General William Henry Harrison had named the fort after Ohio Governor Return J. Meigs.

No one had shown Harrison more support or given more encouragement than the governor of Ohio. Meigs was working feverously to send supply train after supply train to strength Harrison's force.

Meigs worked tirelessly, sending every bit of food and ammunition he could find. He was constantly recruiting new companies of militia to carry those materials to the army in the field.

Harrison had lost the short-enlistment militia, but still had a force of about 1,200 regular infantry at the base. And it was growing fat with supplies for an invasion of Canada.

As the cold winds faded and the soil began to dry, both the Canadians and the Americans waited for the fighting to resume.

It was sure to be bloody.

The last week of April, British General Henry Procter chose to make a preemptive move.

Leaving both Detroit and Amherstburg well-fortified, he moved a large force against Fort Meigs. If he could destroy the Americans' main supply depot, he might just prevent any possible invasion attempts that summer.

With about 600 Royal troops, 462 Canadian Militia, two 24-pounder guns captured from the Americans at Detroit, nine lighter guns, and two gunboats with 9-pounders, he assaulted the American fort.

Tecumseh and Wyandot chief Roundhead came along just to bolster his chances. They brought about 1,300 blood-thirsty savages hoping to enjoy the massacre.

Procter used the natives to surround the fort and harass anyone trying to come or go. Across the river, he set up artillery batteries and began to pound away at the American defenses.

Artillery shells bombarded night and day. From the woods, natives launched fire arrows to try and burn the defensive structures.

Sergeant Charles Cissna and his men were kept busy trying to duck the incoming missiles from one side, and put out the fires coming at them from the other. Four days and nights of continual bombardment will shake a man's faith and courage.

Harrison had constructed the fort well and most of the cannon bombardment was absorbed harmlessly by the earthworks the men had worked so hard to erect.

Though they had been built with curses, threats, and complaining, every man in the force was grateful for them now.

On May 4, a relief force of 1,600 fresh American Infantry arrived at Fort Meigs. Coming through northern Ohio, they had little trouble pushing through the barrier of savages. Harrison now had the upper hand in the siege.

On May 5, a ranger column under the command of Col. William Dudley made a large swing from the left and attacked the British batteries that were pounding Fort Meigs. They stormed those batteries and spiked the guns, ending the bombardment.

But Roundhead's warriors began to fall on the rangers from every direction. The natives used their favorite tactic: jump from hidden places to sting the Americans, then disappear back into the forest. There was no time to fire back at them.

The Kentuckians in Dudley's force tried to follow the Indians into the forest. They hoped to chase them down and break their will. The thick forest undergrowth meant the Americans had to separate into smaller groups.

The warriors fell on the smaller groups and the Kentuckians were decimated.

Now Dudley's group was fighting for their lives to get back to the fort. It was a disaster.

170 Americans died in the confused fighting. Another 550 men were captured. Most of those who were captured were massacred by the savages while being held prisoner.

Only 150 men of Dudley's force of 1,600 made it back to Fort Meigs. But the bombardment was over.

What followed next was amazing to both the frontiersmen and Indians alike.

The American and British officers set down to settle their differences. They negotiated an end to the siege that was basically a stalemate. They counted their captives and swapped prisoners in a very reasonable manner.

The British withdrew on May 9th. The only thing they had accomplished was to make the American soldiers anxious for revenge.

Sergeant Charles Cissna and his company of the 19th Infantry had been kept busy on the perimeter. Watching for cannon shot from their rear, they kept constant vigil against the sudden charges of the natives.

The warriors would strike with surprise and fade back into the woods as soon as they had drawn blood. The war parties kept the harassment up for days.

Numerous times, Sgt. Cissna distinguished himself by keeping his men in the safety of formations, and holding the enemy at bay.

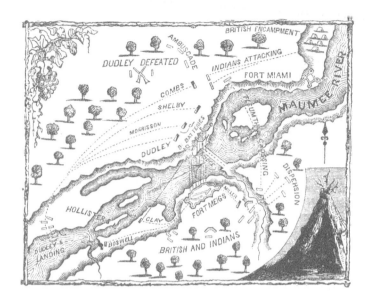

The 26th Infantry from Vermont were among the reinforcement that reported to General Harrison on May 4th and were assigned quarters. They had lost a few men on the march west, and had some holes in their officer ranks.

Because of his actions on the River Raisin, and his service during the siege, Sergeant Charles Cissna was promoted to Ensign (or 3rd Lieutenant) on May 20, 1813.

Field promotions seldom allowed a new officer to stay with his old unit. So Cissna was assigned to a company in the 26th Regiment.

His combat experience was to be used in getting the boys from Vermont ready for the fighting to come. He had a new group of green troops to train.

In June, with the Brits withdrawn to Detroit and Fort Malden, General Harrison left Fort Meigs and started a slow march of his Army north. He left 100 militia men to hold the supplies at Fort Meigs, but his supply train was enormous. He intended to retake Detroit and stay there for a long time.

Tecumseh and Roundhead continued to lay ambush and harass the advancing army.

They had over 4,000 warriors scattered throughout the forests of southern Michigan and northern Ohio. But they were in small groups and none large enough to really deter the mass of advancing Americans.

By September, Harrison had retaken much of Michigan Territory, occupying it in force. He was nearing Detroit and the British were getting nervous.

Charles Cissna was busy with his new company of Vermont men.

They needed his constant guidance for keeping their camp and equipment clean and ready to fight. He fussed over the smallest detail of sanitation and discipline.

It was his job to keep them healthy and ready to fight. But the presence of summer mosquitos and the frequency of "Ague" continued to plague his company.

On September 10, Oliver Perry changed everything. Defeating the British squadron of war ships at Put-in-Bay, Ohio, he shifted the balance of power.

Now the British no longer commanded the lakes. Their far flung forts on the upper lakes could not guarantee that supplies and reinforcement would be able to reach them by ship.

Marching troops and supply trains through the Canadian wilderness was a daunting prospect. The commanders realized that their forts were untenable.

Sensing that he was doomed to fail, the British Commander, General Procter, withdrew his forces from Detroit and Fort Malden.

General Harrison was able to move in and occupy those places without much of a fight. But he was not satisfied with those prizes. Harrison sent his army after Procter's force, chasing them into the interior of Canada.

They met on the River Thames in a massive battle that ended British dominance in Western Canada.

On October 5th, the Battle of Moraviantown along the Thames River would decide the issue.

Harrison's army had caught up with the retreating British. They made a desperate stand. The Americans made an equally desperate attack.

"Remember the Raisin" was the battle cry as Ensign Charles Cissna and his Vermont men charged up the right flank, following the banks of the Thames River.

In this battle the Americans would be victorious. But most significant were the casualties. Tecumseh was killed by the Kentucky cavalry. Chief Roundhead was slain also.

The Indians had lost their mystical leader. Their desire to continue in this war faded quickly after that.

The resistance of native tribes east of the Mississippi ended after the Battle on Thames. Never again, would so large an organized force of natives take the field against the Americans.

"Tecumseh is dead!" echoed across the western theater of war.

The news was celebrated all the way to Washington, D.C. But it was greatly celebrated among the frontier people who were seeking shelter in Chillicothe.

For the first time in months, Charles Cissna and others began to feel there was hope for winning this conflict. It had taken months of preparation and arduous work. Now, a few desperate hours of fighting meant that hope loomed on the horizon.

With the British forces in Upper Canada defeated, and the American base at Detroit retaken, General Harrison did not need the number of men he had.

Parts of the 17th and 19th Infantries were left to hold Detroit. The rest, and the new regiments (including Charles Cissna's company in the 26th Infantry), were sent to the Niagara frontier to help with the fighting there.

This time Ensign Charles Cissna and his men would get a ride instead of having to march through the wilderness. In mid-October, they were carried by the *Niagara* to reinforce the Americans fighting at Erie. They walked into combat almost immediately.

Niagara Campaign Summer 1813

The fighting had not been going well for the Americans. On July 2nd, they had launched a major thrust into Canada and had taken Fort Erie. But it was going to be hard to hold.

The British and Canadians had started construction. But the Americans had assaulted the fort before it was complete.

If its lack of completion made attack vulnerable for the British, it also meant the American defenses would be weak. This incomplete fort was not a safe place to be.

Ensign Cissna and the other reinforcements had barely reached Fort Erie when the British launched a counterattack. This turned into a siege.

The siege meant several things. All of them a deadly threat to Ensign Charles Cissna and his company of men from Vermont.

First it meant that supplies were going to have a very difficult time getting to them from the American fort at Buffalo. Almost immediately, food and ammunition were being severely rationed.

Second it meant that, without warning, the British guns would open up a vicious barrage which might last anywhere from a few minutes to several hours. There was no way to predict when it would come. But every American knew it could start at any moment. The only defense was to stay hidden as close to the ground as possible.

Thirdly, it meant that at any time of day, the British might launch an assault on some part of the line. It was their way of testing the defenses of the American perimeter. And it meant that every soldier on guard duty was in danger of being shot by a sniper.

Ensign Cissna had learned how to survive a siege from his time at Fort Meigs. He put those lessons to work now.

His green troops had no idea of what to expect. Charles Cissna harangued them continually as he ordered them to dig in. They had to be taught when to move and when not to move.

Ensign Cissna could not let his guard down for one moment. He was on alert 24 hours a day, every day of the siege.

In a rush, the men dug earthen berms, and stacked logs, and made piles of stone for fortifications.

Psychologists in the 20th Century say that enduring prolonged bombardment is one of the worst kinds of combat experience. Ensign Charles Cissna was enduring his second.

But it would not be his last.

As winter set in, both sides began to withdraw from the conflict. The fighting season had ended with a stalemate. Now each of the armies went into winter quarters. It was going to be a harsh winter.

A typical winter meant that Lake Erie and the rivers would freeze solid. It also meant that as much as 100 inches of snow could fall to hamper all military operations.

Fort Erie being inadequate and incomplete, the Americans left a small guard to hold it. The rest of the army was withdrawn to the town of Buffalo, New York for winter quarters.

Shortly after the first heavy snow, the British made another attempt on Fort Erie. This time the Americans just walked back to Buffalo without a fight. The Generals did not think it worth making any more effort to keep the fort over the winter.

Ensign Charles Cissna was recalled to Buffalo. As an officer, Charles had a private quarters.

Charles Cissna had a bed!

The rest of his company was housed in an old warehouse. But he was an officer now, and entitled to some comforts.

He had increased in pay and status. As a junior officer, he was frequently dispatched to do errands in the midst of the infamous Erie winter storms. But he had more comfort than he had ever known in army life.

He had earned it by his dedication, courage, and faithfulness to the company he served. While his duty was still hard, he had some comforts to make this winter more endurable.

British storming the Northeast Bastion of Fort Erie, during their failed night assault on August 14, 1814

CHAPTER FOURTEEN
Chillicothe, Ohio
20 July 1813

Governor J. Meigs was at it again.

Another shipment of supplies and been floated down the Ohio River and up the Scioto River, and now lay waiting on the docks at Chillicothe. He would waste no time in getting them on to the Army in northern Ohio.

And the Governor was once again on the street appealing for volunteers to escort the supplies to Fort Stephenson near Sandusky. Following his usual pattern, Meigs introduced newly-appointed Captain Samuel Jones and started him marching up and down the street.

Among the men who fell into ranks and signed the enlistment document was 23-year-old Robert Cissna. He had just been visiting in town from his farm in Fairfield County.

A deeply spiritual man, Robert felt something divine pulling him to enlist.

Robert was the youngest son of Evans and Mary Cissna. They had once been tavern keepers in Pittsburgh.

Captain Evans Cissna had led a company of rangers during the Revolutionary War. Their job was to patrol the remote passes in western Pennsylvania, trying to intercept Shawnee war parties.

Following the war, Evans Cissna lost his taste for farming. He and Mary bought a house on Second Street in Pittsburgh. They soon opened it as a public tavern.

Taverns in small towns were a family enterprise. They were a place where travelers could find a safe night's sleep and a hot meal. Townspeople would gather there to drink and exchange news.

It was also a sort of general store as the proprietor often traded or purchased produce and goods.

But in a city like Pittsburgh, taverns had another character entirely. Hotels kept overnight travelers. Stores bought and traded goods. The tavern was simply a place to drink, to smoke, and to complain about life. It lacked the charm and grace of its country counterpart.

Robert Cissna came along at a time when his parents had run out of passion for child rearing. He was left to raise himself in the rough tavern.

Being tutored in all the adult vices from a very young age, Robert was not the most sociable of youths.

The first public record of Robert is found in an ad placed in the *Scioto Gazette* on 8 October 1806.

"Reward for Return of Robert Cisna. 17 yrs. old; 5'5"; an ill look and an ungovernable temper. He was wearing a roundabout stripped cotton jacket, swans down waist coat, stripped pantaloons, fur hat and new shoes. Brand on the left arm: R. CIS. Fled the apprenticeship of E. Pentland, in Pittsburgh. Believed to have family in Chillicothe. Three Cent reward."

Indeed, Robert had family in Chillicothe. Older brothers Samuel and Thomas had migrated down the Ohio river with their cousin, Stephen Cissna.

Stephen Cissna, "the hero of the Battle of Boston," had brought a large group of the family to Chillicothe in 1799. Stephen opened one of the first taverns in the community.

Cissna's Tavern was one of the political hotspots of the State Capitol. Its patrons were boisterous in their politics, and frequently marched in demonstrations against the governor.

But in 1813, Stephen Cissna's tavern had a much more patriotic flavor. By then, the old soldier had five sons and a grandson invested in this war.

Thomas Cissna was a devoted Christian of the passionate kind of faith. In 1806 he had quickly taken young Robert under his wings and the boy flourished.

The History of Fairfield County, Ohio records that Thomas and Robert Cissna held the first church services of the county in their homes. The book reports that both men could, and frequently did, preach with strong exhortation.

On July 20th, as he listened to the Governor rally the crowd, Robert Cissna felt God was calling him to volunteer.

So, he did.

The next morning Captain Samuel Jones and 79 men of his company were escorting 40 pack horses up the military road towards the Maumee River. There was no time to waste in outfitting the men with uniforms or giving them any training.

Each animal carried four fifty-pound barrels. Half of the barrels contained flour of wheat or corn, and half contained gun powder.

Both were needed by the soldiers fighting in the north.

The military road cut by General Hull was in decent shape from so much travel, and the company was making suitable travel time. But that would change on July 25th.

They were met by a rider racing down the road from the north. He looked tired and desperate. The news he brought explained why.

On July 21st, a new round of fighting had started at Fort Meigs. Tecumseh and a Wyandot chief named Roundhead had brought a force of over three thousand warriors from the Fox, Sioux, Menominee, Ojibwa, Ottawa, Sac, and Winnebago Nations. Fort Meigs was under siege once again. And every road or trail which might lead them to the fort was filled with savage war parties.

Unlike the orderly siege of cannon bombardment brought by the British earlier, this one brought by Tecumseh was like a giant swarm of hornets surrounding the fort.

General Harrison had moved the bulk of his army on towards Detroit. He left only a garrison of 100 militia men to protect the fort. They were badly outnumbered, but the fortifications were well designed.

Tecumseh was hoping to achieve another massacre which would bolster support of his cause among the tribes.

The savages struck repeatedly from any direction and at any time. For seven days, they filled the woods with deathly screams.

It would be impossible for Robert Cissna and the other men to bring their convoy into that post.

Captain Jones was an experienced soldier.

As a private he had fought the Indians in Michigan a year earlier. He understood quite well the danger that lay ahead.

Small war parties would be roaming through the forests for miles around the Fort.

But Samuel Jones was not the kind of man to give up easily. The company immediately abandoned the road. They were easy prey if they stayed in the open.

Captain Jones proposed that they "sneak" their way to Fort Stephenson. They would skirt the Great Swamp and give Fort Meigs a very wide birth, coming to Fort Stephenson from the south.

For the next week, they cut through dense underbrush avoiding all trails. They worked hard to keep all the equipment and animals quiet. They marched in silence and talked only in whispers.

Scouts were continually ahead of them. They camped without fires at night and ate cold meals.

But the worst part was living on the expectation of being discovered at any moment.

On August 3rd, the relief column was nearing their destination of Fort Stephenson. Captain Jones sent two scouts on ahead to determine if it was safe to proceed. The scouts returned with unwelcome news.

On July 30th, a party from the Indian forces around Meigs had attacked Major James Ball and a company of Pennsylvania volunteers just outside Fort Seneca. This was just eight miles north of Fort Stephenson.

Two days later the savages moved on to strike at Fort Stephenson.

Captain Jones weighed the information and guessed correctly at what was happening.

The Indians cannot stay focused long enough for a siege. They had abandoned the attack on Fort Meigs and were now dispersing into smaller bands throughout the area along Lake Erie. They were searching for targets of opportunity.

Captain Jones' company was such a target.

His men were tired. The animals were worn out by the difficult terrain. He decided to gamble everything on one bold move.

They would make a mad dash the eight miles to Fort Stephenson. Half of the men were placed as pickets running through the woods a dozen yards on either side of the column of pack animals. If attacked they would strike back hard, then break off and continue their run for safety.

It took every last ounce of strength the men had. Drained as they were from their arduous journey, they summoned a new burst energy and ran towards safety.

Small groups of savages did find them. Twice they were attacked. After a brief firefight, the Indians broke off, and the Americans ran on.

Every man in the party knew what had to be done. They had to get to the Fort before the Indians could gather enough men to come against them in force.

Robert Cissna was more exhausted than he had ever been in his life, but somehow, he managed to run on. He would never be sure if it were fear or courage that fueled him that day. But he ran on.

They were a frantic sight as they ran through the gates and collapsed on the parade field inside the walls of their destination. Only two of their men had been slightly wounded in the fighting. And the elated feeling of victory overcame them.

That night, as they sat around the fire eating their first hot meal in days, Robert Cissna felt called to praise the God who had saved them.

He was not shy or quiet about it either. In a few minutes, he was preaching quite loudly about how God delivers the righteous from their enemies.

It took two weeks for the woods to empty of the savages. Tecumseh called his Indian army back to Canada to help with fighting there.

Eventually, Captain Jones felt it safe for them to return to Chillicothe. To make the return trip as quickly as possible they rode double on the pack horses.

On September 7, 1813, they returned triumphantly to the Governor's hotel.

Each man was given a discharge certificate and the personal thanks of the Governor. Many of them would use those certificates to apply for pension in their later years. Private Robert Cissna, "preacher" as the men now called him, was one of those who survived long enough to apply for pension.

CHAPTER FIFTEEN
Buffalo, NY
May 1814

It had been a long winter in Buffalo. Average snow fall on the city is 88 inches. But that winter well over 100 inches fell. It made it difficult for the army to keep supplied.

It was not until April when enough supplies had arrived, that the Generals felt they could start a new campaign into Canada.

Ensign Charles Cissna had spent the winter training and nursing his Vermont men of the 26th Infantry. But in May of 1814, their enlistment ran out and his men returned to Burlington.

Major General Jacob Brown granted Cissna's request to transfer back to the 19th Infantry. He became the 3rd Lieutenant of his old company.

Charles was glad to be back with the men from Scioto River country. But the men noticed he had changed. He was an officer in every sense, not the kindly sergeant they used to kid around with.

The American Army crossed the Niagara River and entered Canada again. The months of May, June, and July were spent raiding settlements and towns along Lake Erie.

Ensign Charles Cissna's men were engaged in a slash and burn campaign through the farms of southern Canada.

The strategy was to punish the Canadian militia for having fought against their American cousins. And some of the damage they did was pure retribution for raids the British and Canadians had staged at Black Rock and Buffalo during the winter months.

On July 3 of 1814, General Brown's campaign brought the army once again to Fort Erie.

It had never been an adequate fortification.

During the winter, ice had destroyed what few structures still remained. The few British troops who had been stationed there, simply walked away without a fight as the Americans approached.

Brown ordered his army to dig in and rebuild the Fort. They built two large magazines for ammunition and set to work building ramparts surrounding the fort.

It was obvious to everyone that the British would come back and try to take this fort. It was also obvious that the Americans had no intention of giving it up without a bitter and bloody conflict.

On July 20th, Major General Brown launched a new campaign to dislodge the British from the Niagara area.

Marching a large force in two columns, he proceeded from Fort Erie to Niagara Falls on the Ontario side. It was a sweeping action in full force that was designed to push the Brits back to Lake Ontario.

One company of the 19th Infantry was ordered to march in this campaign.

But it was not the company in which Charles Cissna served as 3rd Lieutenant. He and others would continue building defenses while the main army was marching away.

Fort Erie was to be the main supply depot on the Canadian side of the Niagara River. If needed, it would be a safe place for retreat.

It would be needed.

On July 25th, the American Army emerged from the woods just opposite Niagara Falls. They were met by a large force of Brits with cannon which were well dug in on the heights.

The battle would become known as Lundy's Lane. It was the bloodiest battle fought on Canadian soil, and one of the bloodiest battles of the entire war.

Two well-equipped and disciplined armies stood in neat rows and traded body blows in courageous fashion. The battle ended with both sides withdrawing in complete exhaustion.

So many draft animals had been killed that the American army abandoned its supplies on the field. Every functioning wagon was used to carry wounded back to Fort Erie.

Ensign Charles Cissna watched in grief as the army dragged back over the next two days. The dead counted 174; the missing numbered 28; and another 78 could be confirmed as captured. But the wagons carried 572 seriously wounded men.

The regimental surgeons would be kept sleepless for three days treating them.

Generals Winfield Scott and Jacob Brown were both severely wounded. Scott would not recover in time to serve any further in this war.

Fort Erie instantly became a field hospital.

As the men grew strong enough, they were carried back across the Niagara to hospice in Buffalo, New York. But the army was disheartened.

The British army had withdrawn also, with remarkably similar losses. The battle was a draw.

However, the British reinforced quicker than the Americans. Sensing the Yanks were weak, General Procter launched a counter offensive to retake Fort Erie.

On August 13, the British began a new siege.

It would be the longest and most bloody siege of the entire war. Wave after wave of Brits attacked various parts of the defenses. Every day there was a new assault.

Early in the predawn on the 14th, the Brits attempted a deception.

Creeping towards the American lines, they drew fire. One of the Canadian militia called out in an American accent, "Hey, stop shooting. You are shooting your own men."

Pickets had been placed ahead of the defensive line, and it was reasonable that they were indeed shooting at their own men.

Officer of the line that morning was Ensign Charles Cissna. He ordered the men to stop firing, but he was skeptical.

Walking 20 yard ahead of his line he stood in the dark to wait for the men to come in. Instead of two or three shadows coming through the forest, he identified dozens.

Racing back to the front line, he shouted "It's a trick, boys. Open fire!"

His alertness prevented a breach in the line and certain disaster. Their surprise lost, the Brits and Canadians withdrew.

Charles received high praise for his attention to details.

When the sun rose on August 15th it was to a very fateful day for Ensign Charles Cissna from Chillicothe, Ohio.

He was approaching 31 years of age.

He had not seen his wife and four children in two years. He had endured some of the worst hardship that army life can offer.

This was his third bombardment.

About 3 a.m., a new assault was launched on the Americans. This time the Brits carried scaling ladders and pushed hard.

Large parties of regular British soldiers rushed the right flank. In heavy fighting, they were able to push through the defenses. In just a few minutes, they had captured one of the two American ammunition bunkers. It looked like the entire right flank might collapse.

Ensign Charles Cissna and his men were sent to push back the attack. A highly creative artillery officer came up with a solution. Turning the cannon on his own installation, he fired a single round of "hot shot" into the ammunition bunker.

Immediately the bunker exploded with a magnificent cloud of smoke.

After Action reports stated that more than 300 of the British troops were killed in that single explosion.

The 19th Infantry began pushing the remaining Brits back across the original defensive line. Charles Cissna was pushing his men forward when something slammed him hard against a wall.

In a daze, he tried to get up, and realized he could not.

A musket ball had hit him in the hip, passing clear through his body. It had shattered his pelvic bone and his legs would not work at all.

His part in the war was ended instantly. But Lt. Charles Cissna now began a difficult struggle to save his own life. His men carried him to the surgeon's tent.

Overwhelmed, the surgeon applied bandages to stop the bleeding, then moved on to other wounded.

Sensing that he might die from inattention, Cissna's men grabbed up his stretcher and carried him to the dock. With threats and curses they persuaded the next boat to carry him to Buffalo where he might get better care.

That evening, upon hearing a report of his action, Major General Jacob Brown issued orders promoting Cissna to 2nd Lieutenant.

Lt. Charles Cissna was severely injured. The wounds were life threatening. On several occasions the doctors and nurses gave up on his survival and began to neglect his wounds.

His death would have been certain were it not for a dramatic intervention. Mrs. Charles Cissna left Chillicothe to come to Buffalo and retrieve her husband.

The story of Dorcus Cissna's dramatic rescue of her husband is found in Chapter Eighteen of this volume.

Lt. Cissna would survive. But he would spend the next six months in the hospital. When he died on 7 March 1827 the doctor said it was from complications of those wounds.

CHAPTER SIXTEEN
Chillicothe, Oh
16 February 1814

As was his frequent habit during this war, Governor J. Meigs of Ohio was once again in the street appealing for volunteers. The docks and warehouse at Chillicothe were filled with materials needed by the army in the north. And more were coming every day.

This enlistment would not be just for a few weeks, but for four months. This company of militia would make not one but several trips up and down Hull's military road, moving an enormous amount of material.

Luther Shepherd had been chosen to captain this company. Slowly volunteers stepped forward.

But the response was not as enthusiastic as it had been in past militia enlistments. It actually looked for a while that the effort might fail.

Chillicothe was running out of fresh young men to send off to the fight. The army and militia enlistments had tapped nearly all of the available able-bodied men. It certainly it had tapped all those who were enthusiastic for a fight.

Stephen P. Cissna watched in discouragement as the response was poor. He remembered how badly the fighting had been at his home just south of Detroit. He understood how much these supplies were needed.

But technically, Stephen was still a "prisoner of war." On paper, he had been paroled and was pledged not to serve any further in the conflict.

But he stepped forward anyway.

When they saw him, several others of Captain Brush's "company of prisoners" stepped forward as well.

The issue was no longer in doubt. Captain Luther would have his company to protect the supply trains.

From February 16 until June 16 of 1814, private Stephen P. Cissna made a dozen trips from Chillicothe to Michigan. He never saw another Indian, and the only British soldiers he saw were those held prisoner in Detroit.

The army had constructed a prisoner of war camp just three miles north of Chillicothe. Stephen's company was frequently ordered to bring groups of prisoners on their return trips.

British officers were allowed freedom to enter the town and shop, but enlisted men were not allowed to leave the prison. It was a strange sight for the citizens of Chillicothe to see British soldiers walking their streets.

There were times in the forest when parts of Captain Shepherd's supply train were ambushed by small groups of warriors. Stephen never saw them. But he fully knew the terror at how unexpectedly an attack can occur.

It was four months of long arduous days with very few nights spent in a bed. Later Stephen would say that he could count his hot meals during those months with just one pass over his digits.

Upon his discharge, Stephen P. Cissna found a direction for his life.

He was no longer a single man, available for military service. Returning to Chillicothe, he used his military pay to convince Mary Moore to marry him.

She was the daughter of Dr. Moore.

His father-in-law was so happy to have him in the family that he took Stephen P. Cissna into apprenticeship.

In the summer of 1815, his first child, Amanda Jane Cissna, would be born in Chillicothe. He began practicing medicine shortly thereafter.

When Spencer County, Indiana was opened for settlement shortly after the war, Dr. Stephen P. Cissna would settle in Rockport. Two brothers, Joseph, and David Cissna, would settle there as well.

When he died on 1 March 1841, his epitaph listed a long record of accomplishments. One of those was a brief description of his amazing ability to cure "Milk Sickness."

It was while he was a physician in Rockport that the Lincoln family settled for a brief period in the area.

History of Spencer County also states that he had been the physician for Nancy Hanks Lincoln (mother of Abraham Lincoln).

Many decades later, when trying to identify the grave of Nancy Lincoln, it was determined that she was buried beside Stephen P. Cissna and it was impossible to tell which grave was whose.

CHAPTER SEVENTEEN
Hopkinsville, Kentucky
6 June 1814

Robert Cisney stood reading the enlistment poster on the porch of the general store. "Kentucky Needs Men," it read. The offer was for $8 a month with $20 enlistment bonus. The term required was "the duration of the War."

Kentucky had a long history of disdain and hatred of the savage Indians. Possibly no state sent more militia troops and U.S. Volunteers to fight on the Western Front than Kentucky.

Almost every week a new company was being raised in some part of the state,.

Kentucky had lost a lot of men to the war.

1,000 Kentucky Militiamen had been surrendered by General Hull. And over 300 had perished at the River Raisin Massacre in January of 1813.

Kentucky blood was hot to strike back at the Indians. These volunteers were promised that they were going to strike one final and vicious blow against the native tribes.

Robert Cisney found the recruiting station and was met by Ensign Smith. Without hesitation he signed the enlistment and was assigned his place in the army.

Robert Cisney would serve in the company of Captain Benjamin Desha's 2nd U.S. Volunteer Rifles.

After a quick training camp, they were marched to Detroit to serve in the regiment of Colonel Anthony Butler. They were attached to the Army of General Duncan McArthur.

Robert was 26 years old. His enlistment document provides this description: 5'7", blue eyes, dark hair, fair complexion. He signed on "for the Duration of the War."

Robert Cisney was the son of Stephen Cisney and his wife Patience. Stephen was the only member of the Cisney family to be listed as a loyalist, or Tory, during the Revolution.

In the first year of fighting, many people were still siding with the king against these rebels who were "making problems." Stephen Cisney lived in Guilford County, North Carolina, an exceptionally long way from the politics of taxation in Boston and Philadelphia.

Stephen Cisney was a standing member of the North Carolina Militia and had taken an oath to obey the governor.

In February of 1776 (a full six months before the Declaration of Independence was signed) Stephen Cisney was asked by his neighbors to help the King's soldiers quell an unlawful mob of rebels. Marching to Moore's Creek Bridge to join the Royal Army, Stephen and his company were captured, arrested, and imprisoned at Halifax, NC.

Stephen Cisney and the other men from Horse Pen Creek area were jailed for the term of the Revolutionary War. They never engaged in a single battle, or fired a single shot, but they were prisoners of war, six months before the United States was born.

Following the battle of Yorktown, Stephen and others volunteered to serve in the Continental Army. This gave him the unique status of having fought on both sides of the Revolution.

Following the war, Stephen found it difficult to live with his old neighbors. "Tory" was a label that made life difficult in many ways.

About the year 1800, Stephen and Patience moved their family to a very remote area in Kentucky. They took farmsteads along the Pond River; a few miles north of what would become Elkton, Kentucky.

As new neighbors moved in and settled, the Cisneys were accepted for the quality of their character, not their past politics.

The 2nd Infantry into which Robert Cisney enlisted were U.S. Volunteers.

Congress had decided that militia could not serve more than 6 months, and could not legally fight outside the United States. U.S. Volunteers could be enlisted for far longer; and more importantly, they could fight outside the country's borders.

After a brief training, they were marched straight north. From Hopkinsville, a tobacco road had been established on an old buffalo trail. It would lead them to the Ohio River.

From there, the newly-formed regiment would march to Vincennes. A march that followed the Wabash River through the deep forests would lead them to Fort Wayne. These woods were filled with the bones of both Americans and natives alike, left by the fighting of just two years earlier.

Robert's company marched past the burnt out ruins of numerous villages and trading posts.

By now, the path from Fort Wayne to Detroit had been well worn by the soldiers, pack animals, cannons, and wagons which had gone that way before. The last part of the journey was much easier to transit.

It was at Detroit where they were honed into well-disciplined soldiers. They still wore their own clothes and carried their own rifles. Some of them would be allowed 75 cents per day for providing their own equipment; $1 if they brought their own horse.

Robert Cisney's participation in the war was characterized as "Garrison Duty."

Following his successful campaign against the British and Indians in the fall of 1813, General Harrison had dismissed the militia and divided his army of US Volunteers in half.

The bulk of his army had been carried by to ship to the Niagara frontier. They were emersed in bitter fighting there.

The half of his army which remained with General Harrison had other tasks.

Fort Detroit had to be rebuilt and strengthened. It now replaced Fort Meigs as the central supply base for all the Western border with Canada.

Dangers still threatened Fort Detroit.

There were numerous war parties roaming throughout northern Ohio, Indiana, and Michigan. They were bitter over the loss at the Battle of Thames. They were deeply disillusioned by the death of Tecumseh and other chiefs.

Without unifying leadership, many of the warriors formed parties looking for targets of opportunity. Isolated settlers and travelers were especially vulnerable.

It would take many months to rid the forests of this menace.

A further threat lay far up the lakes. British still held outposts at Fort Michilimachinac (Fort Mackinac) and Fort Edward Augustus. And there were dozens of English trading posts scattered throughout the upper lakes.

All of the British possessions needed a detachment of American troops to come and take possession.

General Harrison divided his forces again, sending a large force to take possession of all British posts on the Upper Great Lakes. Captain Arthur St. Clair, Jr. was leading that expedition. Arthur St. Clair Sr, had served as the governor of the Northwest Territory.

This left the fortifications at Detroit frightfully low on manpower. It was essential that the Americans keep a formidable force at this post, to prevent any counter offensive by either the British or the natives.

That was why Robert Cisney and the other men from Kentucky had been recruited. They were to supplement those troops holding Fort Detroit.

Garrison duty was routine, for the most part. Defenses had already been built before the 2nd US had arrived.

There was maintenance to do. There was a lot of handling of supplies that were first carried to the fort, and then transferred on the troops in the field.

The Kentucky men, because of their experience in the back woods, were frequently dispatched for patrols into the forests surrounding Detroit.

On some occasions, they were dispatched to "punish" an Indian village for their participation in the war. These were the small actions in which Robert Cisney participated.

Though the fighting was small in comparison to battles being fought in other places, they could be just as deadly. A small company of soldiers could just as easily die from an Indian ambush as they could from a canon barrage.

On several occasions Robert Cisney and his company were sent across the river into Canadian territory. These missions had two purposes.

The first was to gather information in case the Canadians were planning to attack Detroit. The second was simply to raid and steal animals and munitions which might one day be used against the American fort.

No dramatic battles or campaigns were attributed to his unit. But they kept secure a dangerous area which had been won only at great loss of life. Though the main fighting had moved on, the dangers of the Michigan frontier were just as real.

Malaria, dysentery, and ambush by savages if you were caught alone in the woods were all very present dangers for these men. Add to that the hardship of being gone from home, and it was far from easy duty.

In January of 1815, the war was over. Andrew Jackson had defeated the British at New Orleans over Christmas.

A Peace Treaty was signed that ended the war in a stalemate. The U.S. and Canada were to move back to roughly the same boundaries they had before the war.

Most of the 2nd U.S. Volunteers were no longer needed. They were discharged at Fort Wayne and sent home. Collecting their separation pay, they were on their own to walk the 550 miles back to Kentucky.

The Army had no choice really. There was no public means of transportation at that time. The Army had no supply trains going in that direction.

There were not really any roads leading them home. Most of the journey would be spent walking down forest trails, eating game they could shoot along the way.

The army offered extended enlistments to a limited number of the men. There was still much of the frontier to protect, even if the government could not afford to pay so many soldiers.

Robert Cisney did not accept discharge. He was transferred to a company under Captain B. Harrison and continued to serve garrison duty for another six months.

Captain Harrison was from Elkton, Kentucky and a close friend of Cisney. In the decades following the war, Captain Harrison would serve as the attorney in Robert's application for the pension.

Harrison, Cisney, and a number of other men from the Pond River and Elkton areas were discharged at

Detroit, Michigan on June 13, 1815. Their regiment was disbanded as a part of the downsizing to a peacetime Army.

Together they made the long walk home. They arrived in the fall, just in time to help with the harvest.

There are a couple of items worth noting about Robert Cisney's later life as it relates to the war.

In 1851, he applied for pension. His file is an exceptionally long one and contains statements from his life-long neighbors along the Pond River. It also has supporting statements from Captain B. Harrison.

In his pension file, at age 80, he reports that he had never known that he was entitled to bounty land, and he is applying for it in old age.

The file also includes an application from Mary Cissna, who claims to be his widow and is asking for survivor's benefits. Mary Cessna was the widow of Robert Cissna from Chillicothe, OH. Robert had served as an assistant teamster with his father, John, while still quite young.

Robert Cisney of Kentucky was asked to confirm her rights as a war widow applying under his service record.

He countered this application with a deposition stating that he was then 81 years old, still alive, and not married. He reported that he had been married twice, but that his second wife had abandoned him 15 years earlier.

Private Robert Cisney/Sisney would spend his final years and die in Muhlenberg County, Kentucky.

His son, Robert A. Cisney, became a Methodist minister and pastored in the community of Rosewood, KY.

For a time, the Post Office in that community was named Cisney, and was located in the store of George Cisney.

EDITOR'S NOTE: For the sake of family historians, Robert Cisney's family tree appears to be as follows. Robert's father was Stephen Cisney of Guilford County, NC. Stephen's parents were John Cessna and Pryscilla Foulke. After John died in York County, PA in 1751, Pryscilla remarried and moved her three children to NC. John's parents were Stephen and Patience Cissna of Carlisle, PA. Stephen's father was the Jean De Cessna who is attributed with bringing the family to America.

CHAPTER EIGHTEEN
Chillicothe, Ohio
6 September 1814

Dorcus Wilcutt-Cissna was not a combatant. But that does not mean she was not a participant. The dearest part of her energy and passion were invested in the national conflict. Like thousands of other wives and mothers, her sacrifice was vital, but often overlooked.

Twice weekly the *Scioto Gazette* published news of the war as it was released by the Secretary of War. After each battle, a list of the dead and wounded would appear.

For many families, it would be the first word they had about their loss. So, each issue was treasured and read with rapt attention. The news had been bad for a month now. Dorcus dreaded the reports which would come in September.

Fighting had renewed in Canada. The Upper Niagara Campaign, as the paper called it; was proving to be a deadly one.

The week before, the paper told how the British had burned Washington, DC. It seemed that the war was turning against the Americans. Already, too many families in Chillicothe had placed black banners in their windows.

Today, what she feared most, finally came.

The news that Dorcus had dreaded was there on the first page. There had been a frightful battle at Fort Erie. The list of the dead and wounded was long. It was terribly long.

Gliding her fingertip over the small type she found what she hoped she would never find. "Lieutenant Charles Cissna; gravely injured August 15 while defending Fort Erie."

"Gravely injured...."

Dorcus understood those words. He had been wounded badly. They struck her like a bolt of lightening.

They hit her so hard that she did not even notice the promotion in rank her husband had received since his last letter.

Charles had survived the wound. But he might not survive the treatment he would receive in an Army hospital. The next report she read might state "2nd Lieutenant Charles Cissna died of his wounds."

Her heart sank low in her chest. What should she do? What could she do?

She ran as fast as she could to "the Barracks."

A few army officers were always on duty, doing much of nothing, really. She grabbed the first one she saw, and shoved the paper in his face.

"Where is my husband?" she demanded of the 2nd Lieutenant.

The officer hesitated a moment because he was not used to being talked to like this by a civilian. But there was enough motherliness about Dorcus that some part of his courage failed and he took a submissive attitude.

"Buffalo. Probably at the Army hospital there," He responded sheepishly.

"I need to go there. Now!" Dorcus stated. "How can I make that happen?"

The officer was overwhelmed at such a request.

Travel during the war was extremely dangerous and difficult. And the place she wanted to go was right at the front of the fighting.

"I am afraid that is just not possible, ma'am. The Army has no way to accommodate wives, either in travel, or in housing after you get there."

"Nonsense! There are plenty of women in this town who went to war with their husbands. You can find a way for me to get there."

"Beg pardon, ma'am, but those wives went with their husbands in the militia. The Regular Army don't allow such a thing. I can't see any way you can get there during the war."

Dorcus could see this junior officer held no options for her. But she was not the kind of woman who was dissuaded easily.

She understood that in a man's world a woman had to play by certain rules to get what she needed.

She would find a way around this little man.

In a great fret, she left the Barracks. Starting for home, her mind would not quit stirring the problem hoping for a solution.

Then one came.

She made a change in direction and her pace quickened. She headed for her father-in-law's place, the Cissna Tavern. He might know what to do. He had some "friends."

The news about Charles had arrived about two hours before Dorcus did. The mood in the place was somber.

Stephen Cissna, the old veteran of the Revolution, was in a dark mood. His mind was also searching frantically for something he might do for his son.

When Dorcus arrived with her request, he seized upon it.

Stephen stood slowly and said, "Come with me, dear."

The look in his eye told the other old men in the place that he was going to stir up some drama. So, they followed along behind just to see the fun.

A short walk took them directly to the Governor's house.

Othniel Looker was the new governor of Ohio. But he was at a political disadvantage.

R.J. Meigs had done such an excellent job at supporting the war effort that the President had appointed him U.S. Postmaster General.

On March 17 of 1814, Looker had been appointed to complete Meigs' term. The Honorable Mr. Looker was serving as the speaker of the Ohio House of Representatives at that time.

He had gotten the job of governor by appointment. But he had to stand for election in the fall. This meant he was vulnerable to public criticism.

Stephen Cissna, Sr. understood the Governor's weakness. They were of the same political party, Democratic Republicans of Thomas Jefferson's brand.

And Stephen had a bit of political influence. He had been a member of the Chillicothe Junto and "Baldwin's Bloodhounds."

The Chillicothe Junto had been the powerful lobby which forced Arthur St. Clair from the Governor's office and pushed through statehood for Ohio.

Though not ranking very high in the group, Stephen had been accountable for much of the veteran's support of the cause. Cissna was recognized not for being one of the formative minds of the party, but for his ability to "rouse the rabble" during an election.

Governor Othniel Looker realized that he should not cross this man.

And an election was just two months away.

Stephen Cissna, Sr. hit the governor's office like a blast from a furnace. Without an introduction, he began his speech.

"I have sent **SIX** sons to fight this war. Two have come home crippled. Now my second oldest child is wounded an in the hospital in Buffalo.

"This state owes my family a great deal! This country owes my family a great deal!"

Governor Looker knew that a lot of people felt that the State owned Mr. Cissna a great deal.

"This young woman here needs to get to Buffalo to care for her husband -- my favorite son! How are you going to make it happen?"

It took Governor Othniel Looker about 15 seconds to weigh his options. If he declined, he would have a very vocal and angry voice against him in the election.

If he overrode the Army's policy, he might have some minor problems from government officials. But if he overrode the Army's policy, he might come off looking like a hero among the local voters.

He chose the latter.

There was a new supply train preparing to leave for Fort Meigs and Detroit. In just a few moments he had written an order to the militia captain to carry Mrs. Cissna with them on the journey.

With a very sympathetic attitude and tone, he carefully handed it to the soldier's wife.

"Madame, if you would, give this note to Captain Barnes in Urbana, he will safely conduct you to Fort Meigs. In three days, he is leading a supply train to that place.

"From there you can get passage on a ship to Buffalo. It is the safest and quickest way I know of for you to get there.

"Give my blessings to your husband. Tell him we are very grateful for what he has done for our country."

By the next morning, Dorcus had hastily provided for her four children: Evans (12), Mary H. B. (8), David (6), and John B. (3 ½).

She placed her brother-in-law, James, in charge of their business affairs until she should return. James was actually her employee in the saddle shop that Dorcus and Charles Cissna had financed.

Dorcus Cissna had not been idle in her husband's absence. While he was at war, she continued to manage all of the business affairs. And she had prospered several existing enterprises, as well as started new ones.

It was Charles Cissna's two younger brothers, James and Joseph, who carried her to Urbana and delivered her to the militia company there.

They had each served under Captain Henry Brush early in the war. Now they would work together to take care of Charles and Dorcus' interests.

It should be noted that the marriage of Charles Cissna and Dorcus Wilcutt was one of the more noteworthy in the community. It was a frequent topic of conversation, not because of their devotion to each other, but because of the contentious competition which consumed the relationship.

Given their history, the town was surprised that Dorcus would choose such a dramatic and expensive response to the news about Charles.

In June of 1801, Charles Cissna and Dorcus Wilcutt met in one of those startling moments which reminds one of the sudden spring storms that Ohio is famous for. The relationship met with a refreshing rush like the promising smell of rain at the storm's first gust.

A spring storm always begins with an exciting rush of air. But it quickly grows in intensity to the point where you can focus on nothing else. It is both exciting and frightening at the same time. It consumes all of your attention and efforts, leaving you wondering where you will find yourself when it passes.

Their love was like that. Strong ... overpowering.

They were married on August 1st.

And from the beginning, their marriage was a partnership like few others. They shared dreams and ambitions. They were at an exciting place and time.

Chillicothe was the Capital of the North-West Territory. Lots of important stuff was going on. Lots of money was changing hands. Enterprise was booming. Statehood was coming.

And Charles and Dorcus shared an understanding and passion for enterprise.

Immediately after their wedding they began to be business partners.

They purchased town lots whenever one came up for distress sale. In the land records, transactions are frequently recorded in the names Charles *and* Dorcus Cissna. This was in a time when wives were seldom mentioned on title transfers.

On February 1, 1802, the couple entered a partnership with Duncan and Ewing to buy a 160-acre farm on Indian Creek. They had only been married six months.

This was not to be a homestead farm.

The Cissnas, Duncan, and Ewing were pioneers in a new prospect called commercial farming. Everything grown on this farm was to be converted into cash. Their home and kitchen garden were in the town.

Samuel Ewing had developed a business plan that they bought into. He would raise and trade for as much flour, salt pork and produce as he could.

Once a year he would float it down the Ohio and Mississippi rivers to New Orleans.

Such goods brought high prices there. And most importantly, they brought cold hard cash, which was in short supply in Ohio.

Working with Ewing, Charles and Dorcus prospered well. They expanded their holdings by converting their cash into land whenever an opportunity arose. Charles and Dorcus made an excellent business team, except for one slight problem.

They were both stubborn and held strong opinions about taking financial risks. Every investment they made required an exhausting amount of debate.

At times, the conflict proved too much.

The best of lovers and friends, the business side of their partnership could be caustic at times. And it was hard to keep this from being noticed in a small town. But the rumors and stories about their personal conflicts did not seem to diminish the couple in the community's eyes.

Once, in 1808, Charles had taken an angry fit and run an ad in the paper that he desired to sell everything: household furniture, home, lots, and all. The town was shocked.

At the time Charles's wife was several months pregnant with his third child. How could he sell everything out from under his family?

Charles did not follow through. But he created quite a stir. He let the ad run for two months as a blatant warning that he was at the end of his patience.

If anything, Dorcus was considered a "woman to be reckoned with" by the men in the community. And the women looked to her as a sort of spokesperson for their gender issues in society.

On July 20th, 1812 (a day that all of Chillicothe held as one of its most important moments in history), Dorcus had emerged as a strong community leader. She and her mother-in-law, Margaret Cissna, had assumed command of a squadron of women.

A new company of militia needed equipment for a quick trip into harm's way. Four young Cissna men were among the volunteers. This was more than any other family in town.

The new company had no uniforms. They also had no munitions or equipment. Together, the town women designed and produced over 100 shirts for Captain Brush's new company of militia. And they had done so in less than 10 hours.

Dorcus was very instrumental in making the pattern which all of the shirts were cut from.

When Charles Cissna had taken another of his angry fits and enlisted in the Army on June 24th of 1812, a month before the Captain Brush event, few people had any doubt that Dorcus would be able to manage things in his absence.

Charles Cissna had enlisted in the regular army to escape his home and wife. That was obvious to everyone in the county.

It was equally as obvious that he was hiding behind some kind of Patriotic duty as a motive. He was simply running away.

A few of the women offered her pity and solace at the absence of her husband. But the men of the community simply directed their business negotiations to her in Charles' absence.

Dorcus had continue to grow all of their enterprises without missing a beat.

In a strange and almost prophetic twist, the absence had made Charles and Dorcus Cissna grow fonder of each other. Through letters they began to appreciate each other more.

Their thoughts were slowed by the letter writing process, and the heated words were eliminated.

They wrote only of the important things. Their love and respect for each other grew stronger with each letter, and with each day apart. When Dorcus reported some new business development, Charles had only praise and not angry concern.

Perhaps the pride which had fueled their stubbornness mellowed through the hardships that each was enduring.

At any rate, their differences seemed unimportant.

Each returned to being the most important thing in the other's life. They were no longer competing for dominance in the marriage. They were both working for the same dream.

That is why Dorcus **knew** she had to go to Buffalo. She had to keep her husband alive. She had to bring him home.

Dorcus understood what most practical people of the day knew. The Army hospital was a much more dangerous place to be than even the battlefield. Infections were rampant.

The close quarters and lack of sanitation enabled such diseases as measles and influenzas to claim more lives than the actual wounds. And staffing was so inadequate that many men just died from neglect.

The lucky ones were those who had a family member come and stay with them. That was the only way to get the kind of attention which precipitated recovery.

Dorcus **HAD** to get to Buffalo.

By constantly pressuring the reluctant officers she encountered, Mrs. Cissna arrived at the docks of Buffalo, New York on 14 September 1814.

It had taken 16 days to get to Buffalo. Ten had been spent traveling the Military Road from Urbana to

Fort Meigs, Ohio. The road would accommodate supply wagons by now, but did not allow the swift or comfortable travel of commercial stage lines.

After two days of waiting, the commander at the fort reluctantly placed Dorcus on a packet ship carrying dispatches to Buffalo. Among those letters was an official complaint that the Governor of Ohio had lost his mind and was sending a woman by military transport.

Dorcus spent most of a day searching the city trying to find her husband. There was not one single hospital. The Army had commandeered dozens of whare houses, stables, and homes to serve as places of convalescence. Some were places just for surgery. Some were places where men were sent to die.

None of them had adequate staffing or food.

When Dorcus did find her husband, she barely recognized him.

Charles was filthy, unshaven, and emaciated. The poor quality and unpredictability of food service was slowly starving him to death. He had bed sores that were greatly infected from lack of someone to turn him in his bed.

It was obvious from the attitude of the staff and those patients around him, that Charles was being allowed to die.

The nature of his wound was such that he would probably never walk again. The bullet had passed clear through his body, shattering his hip, and nicking his ileum. It was too high in his body for the doctors to do their usual amputation.

The slow leaking of fluids from the intestine into his body cavity had caused infection throughout his lower abdomen. He was racked with fever.

Twice the doctors had reopened his wounds and flushed his abdomen with vinegar and water. It was the only antibiotic available to them.

But each time the wounds closed; infection would begin to build again. There was very little help they could offer him.

Now they had given up on any further interventions.

Dorcus realized that it was a miracle he was still alive. Though confused with fever, Charles recognized his love, and responded quickly to her presence.

She began to work furiously to correct the circumstances.

Recognizing that with the bullet holes closed, his body had no way to release the fluids caused by the infection, she found a doctor and harassed him mightily until he agreed to reopen them.

His reluctance was understandable. With no medicine for pain, and no anesthetic available in those days, the procedure was going to cause great trauma to a very weak man. Another surgery would certainly kill him, and do so in a very painful way.

But Dorcus was insistent.

Once reopened, the wounds could allow the fluids to drain. To keep the wounds open, Dorcus had to carefully pack them with long strips of muslin soaked in vinegar.

This had to be done several times a day. Mrs. Cissna tended this task religiously, giving Charles lots of emotional support with every procedure.

At first, the unpacking and packing of the would was as painful as the surgery. Charles screamed in pain at every touch.

In this way, Dorcus let his wounds heal from the inside out. The infection began to lessen. His fever subsided. His pain faded as well.

Dorcus had brought enough cash to hire a private room. She moved Charles from the hospital. Her persuasive nature coerced a doctor into making visits to that room.

She began to manage everything. She provided hearty and regular meals. She never let her husband lie on the bedpan for hours as the hospital staff had done.

She turned him frequently in the bed. And she gently washed all of his infections numerous times per day.

In time, his body began to respond the way his spirit had.

It would take four weeks of packing and draining his wounds for them to close completely. When he had healed enough, she had him carried to the front porch and let him see life passing him by.

Dorcus had guessed correctly that watching people rush to and fro in their business adventures would stir something in him.

He began to discuss the current markets, and eventually even politics. The first time he cussed about a politician, she knew her husband was coming back.

Charles began to talk like he might not walk again.

Dorcus used her innate stubbornness to convince him to try. She hired a craftsman to make him a pair of crutches.

One leg would never operate the way it was supposed to, but with a little training, he was able to pull it along and make it hold his weight as he moved.

It was an awkward walk, but he could move forward under his own power. And he was ready to go home.

The doctor in charge of the hospital was impressed at Charles Cissna's recovery. He made notes of things that Dorcus had done for her husband. And he recommended the army grant Charles Cissna a furlough to continue his healing at home.

Charles and Dorcus returned to their home in Chillicothe a few days before Christmas in 1814.

Their love and partnership would never again be tested and strained as it had before. Now they knew how very much they needed each other.

Though they had never doubted each other's love, they had doubted selfish intentions to control the other.

It would never be a problem for them again. She needed him. He needed her. They both understood that fully.

Their next child, Charles Cissna, Jr. was born exactly nine months after their return to Chillicothe.

Julia Ann followed in 1817. Samuel James Cissna was born in 1822. Elizabeth Ann arrived in 1824.

And their last child Eliza Jane was born on November 20, 1827. Her father had died seven months earlier.

Dorcus was 43 years of age when her last child was born, and she was widowed.

Such was the quality of woman that built America. Dorcus Wilcutt-Cissna lived a life a heroic as any of the men who fought in the War of 1812.

CHAPTER NINETEEN
Utica, Mississippi
Sept 15, 1814

"HallllooooooYaaaa!"

The boys around Utica were a cavalier bunch. Plantation work was intense for only a few weeks in the planting, and again in the harvest. Most of that work was done by the slaves.

Young white men were left just to ruminate and postulate.

Most of their passion was focused not on the work, but on gambling, raising/racing horses, and hunting. They were immensely proud of their dogs and steeds.

Andrew Jackson was well known in the community. Several times a year he would come to town in a large flourish.

Usually, he was transporting slaves from Tennessee and Southern Kentucky to be sold at the markets in Natchez. And Jackson could always be counted on for a horse race. He was quite proud of the thoroughbred that he rode.

The sons of local plantation owners all fashioned themselves to be gallant young knights, born in the wrong century. Dense forests separated the plantations from each other.

It was customary practice for the young men to release a startlingly loud war cry as they rode swiftly past their neighbors.

Each man had his own distinctive yell so his neighbors would know he was present even if they could not see him through the trees. The sound of their unique cry would echo through the tall pines of the forest.

On this occasion, the cry came from young James Cessna. He reined his mount to a dusty halt in front of Doherty's Plantation Supply store.

"Everything you need for the Finest Plantation," the store claimed.

The crowd had already gathered and James was one of the last to arrive. He was expecting an exciting new horse race to participate in, or at least to bet on.

Young Cessna was taken aback by the mood of the crowd. The usual gay mood was gone from his friends.

For weeks, they had been getting news about Andrew Jackson's campaign against the Red Stick Creeks. "Old Andy" had been on a campaign of extermination in the eastern half of Mississippi. This was land that would soon become Alabama.

The Creek and several lesser tribes had responded to Tecumseh's call for a war to drive the whites back into the sea. In August of 1813, a large war party of "Red Stick" Creek warriors attacked Fort Mims on the southern reaches of the Alabama River.

This was not an attack to defeat the whites. It was to exterminate them according to the prophecy preached to them by Tecumseh two years earlier.

Over 500 of the militia and settlers were killed and scalped. A very few were taken as slaves. After their victory, the Red Sticks "razed the surrounding plantations.... They slaughtered over 5,000 head of cattle, destroyed crops and houses, and murdered or stole slaves."

In response, Governor Willie Blount decided to raise 5,000 militia for a three-month tour of duty. They would invade Alabama and Mississippi and punish every Indian village they came to.

A force of 2,500 men from Western Tennessee formed a militia army under Colonel Andrew Jackson with the assignment to "repel an approaching invasion ... and to afford aid and relief to Mississippi Territory".

He also summoned a force of 2,500 from East Tennessee under Major General John Alexander Cocke.

Although technically Cooke was the highest ranking officer, it was Andrew Jackson who assumed leadership. His goal was clear.

Jackson led his army into northern Alabama with the purpose of destroying every Indian family he might find. It completely escaped his wisdom that at this time, the Creek Nation were in the midst of a civil war.

Those Creeks who were waging the Red Stick War were in a minority. Most wanted peace. Their civil dispute grew so heated that a large branch of the tribe broke off from the main. They began to call themselves Seminoles and relocated in Florida under Spanish rule.

None of that stopped Jackson's army from a vicious campaign of revenge. He ordered his men to kill every Indian they came upon, regardless of age or sex.

One of Jackson's captains, a young man named Davey Crocket, was so disgusted with the slaughter that he filed complaints.

At one point, Jackson arrested Crocket and threatened him with Court Martial. Crocket and a large number of the militia from Eastern Tennessee simply quit and went home when the three month enlistment was over.

After a bloody campaign that lasted over a year. Jackson had nearly beaten all of the tribes into submission, or left their bodies in the forest.

Before he could settle back onto his plantation outside Nashville, a new threat was presented.

The British had landed at substantial force at Pensacola, Florida. They were building a strong new fort, to use as a base of operations against the Americans in the south.

Technically, Pensacola was Spanish territory. Having no love for the Americans, the Spanish Governor decided to turn a blind eye to the British presence.

It was a classic case of "the enemy of my enemy, must be my friend." Still, when pressed through diplomatic channels, the Spanish Governor claimed he had no knowledge of the British presence.

From this new fort, the Brits were arming the Creek Indians to wage war against the Americans from the south.

It was a repeat of the strategy used by the English commanders along the great lakes. Provide guns, ammunition, food, and rewards for scalps; and let the savages do the fighting for you.

Thomas Hinds was standing on the porch of Doherty's Plantation Supply store. Several hundred men stood silently in front of the building. They listened as Hinds made a dramatic plea for helping Andrew Jackson.

Hinds painted a picture of the great danger they were in.

Andrew Jackson was a man they knew well, both in person and by reputation. His successes as a military commander were well documented in the local newspaper.

Hinds's message held three hot buttons for every one of the Mississippi gentlemen. The British were building a fort in their back yard. They were arming the Creeks to bring war among their farms. Andy Jackson was asking for their help!

By the time he was finished, every man in Hinds County could imagine hoards of Creek warriors descending on their plantations.

Jackson needed more men for the fight.

The governor of Mississippi was raising a new army to send to his aid. It would rendezvous and organize at the Territorial Capitol of Washington just a few miles from Natchez.

John Doherty had been asked to serve as captain and raise a company of soldiers. As Col. Thomas Hinds stepped back, young Doherty stepped forward. He needed volunteers.

There was never a doubt as to what kind of company it would be.

It would not be infantry.

"Utica has some of the finest horses and horsemen in the country. We need to send a company of dragoons," Doherty shouted from the porch of his father's business.

His call was met with wild shouts and cries from the crowd. Each man released the loudest version of his personalized war cry. They were hoping that the noise could be heard all the way to Parliament in London.

Among the first to step forward was John Cessna Neel. He had already served an enlistment early in the war. On that occasion, he helped build the fortifications at Baton Rouge.

Now when asked to enlist for six more months, he did not hesitate.

Joining him were two cousins, James and Charles Cessna. All three boys were being raised as brothers at the plantation of Colonel Charles Cessna, just half a dozen miles north of Utica.

John Cessna Neel was the son of Aaron and Mary Cessna Neel. The Neels lived several miles northwest of the Colonel's plantation. But young John managed to spend most of his time with the old gentleman.

The attraction was obvious. The old Colonel was raising four boys without the limiting influence of a woman. The old bachelor had agreed to raise Charles, Culbertson, William, and James Cessna. Or perhaps, they were the ones taking care of him.

It is uncertain if these young men were grandsons or nephews of Colonel Charles Cessna, the Revolutionary War hero. What is certain from court documents is that the old man considered them heirs of his estate.

The old Colonel tended to spoil the three boys. Col. Cessna had begun life in Cumberland County, Pennsylvania.

During the Revolution, he had served as Representative from Bedford County, Purchasing Agent for the Pennsylvania Public Safety Committee (state war department), and as a Major of one of the regiments of militia erected to protect the county.

Following the war Col. Charles and his brother Major John Cessna fell victim of vicious politics. Newly freed of English rule the new country sought to fill the void of power left by the revolution.

Charles had simply moved to Greene County, Georgia. Then he moved again to Muhlenberg County, Kentucky. And finally, he became one of the earliest settlers in Utica, Mississippi shortly after 1802.

Each of his moves seems to have been precipitated by some political discord.

But Colonel Charles Cessna was a man of means, and his reputation made him sought after by the government authorities which were trying to settle new lands. In each move, Charles received sizeable grants of land, in reward for his service during the Revolution.

Former military officers made good community builders.

The home of Col Charles and Elizabeth Cessna was not palatial, but certainly held far more luxuries than the average home.

The boys had few responsibilities. They had ample monies to have magnificent steeds and gentlemanly costumes.

Household slaves managed their more mundane needs.

The boys were like the Three Musketeers as they competed for dominance in what passed for society in rural Mississippi.

Below is a typical home constructed by plantation holders in Utica at the time Colonel Charles built his.

Now they were going off to war together. They could not have been more excited or optimistic.

John C. Neel told them that it was unlikely they would actually see any fighting. He expected another tour of service like his first.

Interestingly, John Shanks, who had been an officer in 1812, enlisted in this cavalry unit as a private.

Doherty's Company of Mississippi Cavalry galloped the 100 miles to the Territorial capitol. There they would be incorporated into a large regiment called Hind's Dragoons.

Each man brought his own equipment. Each brought at least one pistol; two if he had them.

Many brought swords to use in cavalry charges. Some of these were holdovers from the Revolution. Others were more decorative types which were sold by the European importers in Natchez and New Orleans.

Hinds' Dragoons were a gallant, boisterous, unruly, and excited mob as they set out to meet General Andrew Jackson's army at Mobile. There being few roads, the company made its way along old Indian and Buffalo trails.

It was not long before first blood was drawn. But it was not the casualty they had anticipated.

On the trip from Utica to Washington, Mississippi, Charles' prized horse was lost. While negotiating a swamp, it had broken its leg and was put down.

Charles Cessna rode double with his brother the rest of the way to the Territorial Capitol. Cousin John C. Neel carried his saddle and other equipment.

At the rendezvous, the trio received heart-breaking news.

No horses were to be had without an exorbitant price. And the boys had not thought to bring more than a few dollars with them. Charles would not find a substitute mount.

The young lad had two options. Either he could go back home, or agree to serve in an infantry company. He chose the latter.

Charles Cissna would march to war as an ordinary soldier in the company of Captain Samuel Bullen, under command of Lieutenant Colonel Peter Perkins.

Private Charles Cissna marched the remaining 250 miles to Mobile, their first engagement.

James Cessna and John C. Neel did not take a straight road to Mobile. The dragoons covered well over 500 miles in making the trip.

The cavalry was continually sent out to gather intelligence of what lay ahead and around the army.

When the three lads could spend an evening together around a fire, they vied to see who had the toughest duty in their adventure.

At the same time this new army of Mississippi Volunteers was being organized in Washington, the British were moving into Pensacola, a sleepy fishing village, in the Spanish-owned territory of Florida.

Without any objection from the Spaniards, the Brits began to build forts there.

The intention was to use Pensacola as a base to invade the U.S. from the South. Immediately the English began to arm Indians and free blacks to fight against the Americans. News that they were freeing slaves, and arming them to go back and kill their masters created an even greater panic.

Andrew Jackson saw the danger immediately and began his march to that place.

On September 12th, the British launched an attack on the American fort at Mobile. A force of 225 Royal Marines, supported by a host of Indian allies, landed a short way from Fort Charlotte, and began an advance.

If the English could capture the American Fort, all of Mobile Bay could be used to unload arms and ammunition to open a southern front in this war.

Fort Charlotte held a commanding position on the Mobile Bay.

The English officers knew it would be impossible to take the fort by bombardment of ships in the bay. But the British did not neglect that aspect. Five gunships sailed into the bay and began a siege.

Pounded from gun ships in the Bay, and with a force of British marines threatening them from land, the small force at Fort Charlotte was in trouble.

Added to those threats, thousands of warriors now infested the forests around Fort Charlotte, making it difficult for any help to come from land.

The Mississippi Volunteer Infantry were on foot and still a week away.

But Hind's Dragoons could make that distance in a hurry. So, the cavalry unit of James Cessna and John Cessna Neel was ordered to reinforce the fort.

The Bay of Mobile proved too shallow for the British gunboats. The largest was run aground. Her captain decided to blow her up instead of letting the Americans have her.

Riding in close formation, Hind's Dragoons seemed too strong a force for the Indians to attack. They passed through that hazard without any problem.

In just a few days, the Cessna cousins and their company were in the fields in front of the American Fort.

The appearance of the Mississippi Cavalry convinced the British Marines that they should have a change of heart, and they retreated.

The army from Mississippi moved easily into Fort Charlotte at Mobile Bay and relieved the troops there.

They arrived in time to receive two awfully bad pieces of news.

The first was that the British were well dug in at Pensacola and a hard fight waited for them. This time, it would be the Americans trying to assault a very well constructed fort.

The second was news that a British army had burned the Capitol and White House buildings in Washington, DC.

Parliament had thought it would humble the Americans. But most of the country received the news the way the Mississippi boys at Mobile did.

In reality, American resolve for this war was steeled by the news about Washington, DC.

With his reinforcements from Mississippi, Andrew Jackson now had a formidable force. The cavalry was set to work immediately.

Roaming the rich farms and Spanish towns along the Gulf coast, they found ample supplies to keep the army well fed. The mounted soldiers were able to negotiate the salt marshes, and gather intelligence on the positions of the British.

The first week in September, Andrew Jackson and the Southern Army of America invaded the Spanish territory of Florida.

The Spanish governor could not decide if he should defend his province or not. After all, the Americans had not come to attack him, but to fight the English trespassers. (The enemy of my enemy is my friend.)

Jackson's army was able to walk into Pensacola with only a small fight on November 6th.

Marching from the east (to avoid cannon fire from the Spanish and British forts), the cavalry met with light resistance.

In the middle of town, however, a line of infantry had formed a blockade. It was supported by a battery of cannon. They opened fire on the American cavalry and infantry with cannons loaded with grapeshot.

Hind's Dragoons charged forward in a rush and their horses leapt over the barricade. The English soldiers were routed and retreated to their ships.

Several Americans were wounded. And there was one casualty which has a bearing on this story.

Private James Cessna had his prized horse shot from under him. Gravely wounded, the animal had to be "put down" in the midst of the fighting.

Remembering the plight of his brother Charles, James broke free of the battle and entered the town with a mission.

Before returning to his company, he had "found" another mount for himself.

It was not entirely adequate, but it would keep him from becoming an infantryman.

The next morning, General Jackson intended to attack Fort San Miguel, which was held by the British. The army prepared for a pitched battle against crack British troops.

But before dawn, the Royal navy and marines blew up Fort San Miguel and sailed away.

The decision was made that it just was not worth the fight to hold it. At least that is what the American soldiers thought.

Andrew Jackson knew different. The English were amassing a large force in Jamaica. They were recruiting soldiers from all of the Caribbean colonies for a massive invasion of New Orleans.

Jackson left most of the Mississippi Militia to hold Pensacola and Mobile and raced towards New Orleans.

Arriving at the largest city east of the Appalachian Mountains, Andrew Jackson was shocked to see that no preparations had been made for defense.

Indeed, the people of the city saw little need.

Having been under the Spanish, the French, the British, and the now Americans, they were just not overly concerned about who might claim them next.

Life seemed to go on as before with each new conqueror.

In fact, of all of their conquerors, the people of New Orleans liked the Americans the least and were perfectly content with their being driven away.

Jackson realized he would get extraordinarily little help from the people of this city.

He sent word for help frantically in every direction. He sent envoys to negotiate with several thousand pirates at Barataria. And General Jackson decided he needed the troops he had left behind at Pensacola,

On Dec 20, 1814, Col. Hinds arrived with his Mississippi dragoons. They had ridden 250 miles in four days. The men and horses were exhausted.

James Cessna and John C. Neel had arrived in time to participate in the largest and most important battle of the war.

On December 24th, General Keane arrived a day's march from New Orleans with a force of about 1,800 British troops.

They camped along the east bank of the Mississippi. But they would get no sleep that night.

Andrew Jackson immediately ordered every fighting man at his disposal to attack the British camp. The entire night was filled with a fierce battle.

Without the moon it was so dark that the armies were totally confused. It was hard to know who was fighting whom.

Hind's Dragoons played a significant role in this battle. Swiftly they rode around the enemy's camp, staging short and vicious attacks from every direction.

For the next two weeks, The Cessna cousins and the other dragoons were continually in the field. They raced swiftly through the surrounding swamps to gather information about the movement of British troops.

They staged guerilla style attacks whenever possible on supply and couriers of the British. James Cessna and John Cessna Neel were in constant motion and continual danger the entire time.

They had little opportunity for sleep. They had little opportunity for a hot meal. Their lives were a continual state of alertness, with death waiting around the next bend of the trail.

General Jackson withdrew three miles from the British camp. He chose the Chalmette Plantation and dug in for an all-out fight.

Jackson began to assemble the most amazing fighting force one could imagine.

Defense works several miles long were erected from every material they could find.

Manning the "wall" were frontiersmen from Tennessee and Kentucky, freed blacks, slaves, creoles, Choctaw warriors, French and Spanish speaking farmers, and fishermen. Among them was a terrifying assortment of pirates under Captain Jean Lafitte.

Among his most valuable tools were the incredibly accurate cannoneers from the pirates. His second greatest weapon was the lightning-fast effectiveness of Hind's Dragoons.

On January 8th, 1815, the British felt satisfied that they had landed sufficient amounts of supplies and men.

Looking across the field at the menagerie of soldiers that were waiting for them, the British soldiers were confident that it would be a short skirmish. They were wrong.

Sharpshooting frontiersmen had no trouble decimating the pretty rows of red coats marching toward them across the fields. Their weapons could reach out and bring death at three times the distance available to the British Brown Bess muskets.

The accuracy of the pirate cannoneers was able to harass and disorient the British Officers who were trying to command the action from far behind the lines. As the red coated soldiers got closer, the pirates switched to shooting grapeshot from their cannon. Great swaths of British soldiers fell.

The harassing stings of Hind's Dragoons against their flanks kept the Brits grouped together in the center. It all proved too much for the English Army.

The few English soldiers which reached the ramparts were quickly dispatched by the frontier fighters.

At the end of that day, January 8th, the British had lost over 2,000 men, killed or wounded. The Americans had suffered only 71 casualties, and only 13 of those had died. The Brits soon withdrew from Louisiana completely.

Ironically, peace had been declared between the Americans and Great Britain a full two weeks before the Battle of New Orleans.

But word would not reach Andrew Jackson for several weeks.

Charles Cessna and his company of infantry at Fort Charlotte would continue on garrison duty until their six months' enlistment was complete. Given $53.95 in separation pay, he walked his way home to Utica.

John C. Neel and James Cessna continued to serve in Jackson's army. They had three months to sample the worldly delights of New Orleans.

The amazing city offered little comfort to the soldiers who had to sleep in tents among the swamps surrounding it. Hundreds of the American soldiers fell victim to the mosquitos and snakes. More died from the living in the swamp than from the fighting of January 6th.

On March 28th, 1815, the Cessna cousins and their friends from Utica were discharged and allowed to go home. They each received $120.40 as separation pay.

James received an additional $75 as compensation for having his horse killed under him at Pensacola.

The newly released cavalry men were on their own to make their way back to Hinds County.

CHAPTER TWENTY
U.S. War Department
Washington City
June 1815

At the end of the war, Congress disbanded most of the military forces they had assembled for the war.

Popular feeling was that a militia of freemen could always be called upon to defend this country.

While many congressmen felt that a small military force was all that the country needed, others insisted that the ranks of professional soldiers had to be larger than it had been before the war.

Wiser mind reminded the Congress that it had simply taken too long to mobilize and train an effective fighting force when the National Emergency developed in 1812.

In fact, in the early years of the war Great Britain had nearly defeated the Americans. They were much more prepared because they had a large standing force of American troops.

The miserable defeat of General Hull at Detroit had demonstrated the need of an experienced officer corps.

It was in this atmosphere that a great and rare honor was bestowed on Lieutenant Charles Cissna of Piketon, Ohio.

As the War Department chose which few officers would be retained for peacetime duty, Charles was selected. He received orders making his promotion to 2nd Lieutenant his permanent rank.

The letter also asked when he might be ready to return to duty.

He was greatly humbled by the letter which bestowed this honor on him.

But his wounds during the war left him far too disabled to continue in service.

Charles Cissna carefully drafted his response to the War Department. A photocopy of it is below.

Charles Cissna remained a cripple for the rest of his life. He could not move himself without the aid of others.

Within twelve years, the wounds he received at Fort Erie would account for his early death.

The Historical Register and Dictionary of US Army, complied by Francis B. Heitman offers the following entry:

Charles Cissna of Ohio. Ens in 26th Inf on 20 May 1813, Trans to 19th Infantry 12 May 1814, bvt 2 lt 15 Aug 1815 for dist der in defense of Ft. Erie UC; Hon discharged 15 June 1815; died 7 Mar 1827.

Made in the USA
Middletown, DE
17 September 2022

10693336R00116